Seek The Motive And Intentions Of The Heart!

By:

Anthony Montoya

Seek The Motive And Intentions Of The Heart!

By

Anthony Montoya

Copyright © 2015, All Rights Reserved
Printed in The United States of America

Published By:

ABM Publications
A division of Andrew Bills Ministries Inc.
PO Box 6811, Orange, CA 92863

www.abmpublications.com

ISBN: 978-1-931820-66-0

DEDICATION

I would love to dedicate this book to my family & friends, who helped me through my walk of life. I would love to thank, David, Lupita, Nathaniel Sanchez & family, Pauli & Jack Taniguchi, My brothers Adrian Calderon and Robert Briseno for aiding me for shelter when I was living in my car. Also Prophet Mark, Sharon Sohmer, Mama McGee and Stevie. Prophetess Karen & Gilbert Bowser aiding me for shelter and food for several months. Prophetess Marie Santilliano for aiding me with intercession one night when I was in urgent need of a demonic attack, I was not supposed to be attending certain meetings where these spirits of warlocks and witches were even though they were apostles and prophets, I called Marie at midnight, I was being choked by a python spirit through a false prophet who astro projected out of his body and controlled another person to walk over to me and lay hands on me. She called it out within seconds and then rebuked me and corrected me. Prophetess Cynthia from Riverside California, Prophetess Cynthia from Glendale California. Prophetess Veronica from Rialto California, she called me one night while I was being attacked by the spirit of rejection & abandonment a dark heavy cloud, haven't spoke to her in three years and she called out of know where and broke the stronghold off me.

I would also like to thank, Prophetess Lily & Luis Avila, Sara, Denise, Prophet Brian & Claudia. Prophet Andre Hardin & Wife Pamela, Apostle Al Fornis for a major deliverance and breakthrough, Prophetess Deanne, Prophet Carlton LaGrange. Prophet Donnie from Louisiana who prophesied to me in detail and stated I had to wait 9 more months, and then I was removed from the burden of being homeless. Prophet Garret Lloyd, Prophet Michael Hodges & Family taking me through heavy healing and Deliverance. Prophet Hue Fortson taking me through heavy deliverance. Prophetess Stacy Yada, Apostle David Vizcara for aiding with money and material things. Prophet Alex & family, Prophetess Anita Morvac for her intercession, Prophetess Cindy from Upland California. Prophetess Young for her hospitality from Covina California. I would love to thank my brother Andrew from Corona California, Albert Garcia & family, Monique, Laura for aiding me food and money. Also I would love to thank Juan Valdez for shelter and food for several months. Prophet Evan walker for breaking a certain stronghold an affirming that it was over. My Parents Mary & Santiago for their tender loving care and hospitality.

TABLE OF CONTENTS

ACKNOWLEDGEMENTS

It is with much excitement and honor that I get the opportunity to acquaint you with my friend Anthony Montoya. In his unique style he reflects authentic leadership, tempered by a deep compassion for the lost. In this age of religious phonies and spiritual apathy, Anthony does not compromise the unfailing word of God.

His passion and exuberance for God is infectious; Challenging Christians to draw closer to God and take the Bible serious. During a time I was seeking a speaker for my Ministry, God said to me "call Anthony". God used Anthony to confirm some important future Ministry events that He had already spoken to me about. For the reasons above, and others that followed, I look forward to future Ministry with Anthony where his gifts will edify and be a blessing to the Body of Christ.

Lilly Avila
Rays of Glory Ministries, Inc.

In all the 19 years that I have known Anthony Montoya, he has been very poised and consistent. He's a man I know who rightly divides the Word of truth. He carefully hears from the Holy Spirit and he speaks as the Spirit gives him the utterance. I highly recommend his work to any reader out there.

Lloyd Nsek
Author of *"Christianity the End of Spiritual Confusion"*

CHAPTER 1

Shalom Saints let's begin with the continuing of his wonderful revelations of his word. Now my previous books spoke of A Cloud, to be caught up and to become his presence also, when you are caught up   you become rain. The mystery speaks of his words of revelation and his voice, you communing with him and him with you. Job 37:

[2] Hear attentively the noise of his voice, a sound that goeth out of his mouth. [5] God thundered marvelously with his voice; great things doeth he, which the great rain of his strength (His word). Verse 6"For He says to the snow, 'Fall **Object** on the earth'; (Snow is white, he shall make us white as snow).

And [He speaks] to the showers and to the downpour [of His mighty rains], 'Be strong (Revelation of his word). Verse 7 "God seals (brings to a standstill, stops) [by severe weather] the hand of every man, (**2091** zahab zaw-hawb' from an unused root meaning to shimmer; gold, figuratively, something gold-colored (i.e. yellow), as oil, a clear sky:-- gold(-en), fair weather) walking in truth in heart and soul as oil, a clear sky having the mind of christ not mans twisted teachings.

That all men [whom He has made] may know His work [that is, His sovereign power and their subjection to it].

By the breath of God frost is given: and the breadth of the waters is straitened.[11] Also by watering he wearieth the thick cloud: he scattereth his bright cloud: [12] and it is turned round about by his counsels: that they may do whatsoever he commandeth them upon the face of the world in the earth. Frost in Greek means (and transparent), he wearieth a thick cloud (Hard headed Prideful); weary in Hebrew means to decay or wax old. This also speaks of the scripture in Jude.

Jude 1: [10] But these speak evil of those things which they know not: but what they know naturally, as brute beasts, in those things they corrupt themselves.

[10] Woe unto them! For they have gone in the way of Cain, and ran greedily after the error of Balaam for reward, and perished in the gainsaying of Core.

[11] These are spots in your feasts of charity, when they feast with you, feeding themselves without fear: clouds they are without water, carried about of winds; trees whose fruit withereth, without fruit, twice dead, plucked up by the roots;

[12] Raging waves of the sea, foaming out their own shame; wandering stars, to whom is reserved the blackness of darkness forever.

Yahweh goes on to say he scattereth his bright clouds; they do whatever he says when he speaks to them us who are obedient. Job 37:[13] He causeth it to come, whether for correction, or for his land, or for mercy. [19] Teach us what we shall say unto him; for we cannot order our speech by reason of darkness. Those who are in darkness or twisted doctrine cannot understand the cloud or his word or his revelations. Our ascension as Immortality her on earth now, The Tabernacle age.

1 Corinthians 15:42 [42] It is the same way with the resurrection of the dead. Our earthly bodies are planted in

the ground when we die, but they will be raised to live forever. [43] Our bodies are buried in brokenness, but they will be raised in glory. They are buried in weakness, but they will be raised in strength. [44] They are buried as natural human bodies, but they will be raised as spiritual bodies. For just as there are natural bodies, there are also spiritual bodies.

[45] The Scriptures tell us, "The first man, Adam, became a living person."[h] But the last Adam— that is, Christ—is a life-giving Spirit. [46] What comes first is the natural body, then the spiritual body comes later. [47] Adam, the first man, was made from the dust of the earth, while Christ, the second man, came from heaven. [48] Earthly people are like the earthly man, and heavenly people are like the heavenly man. [49] Just as we are now like the earthly man, we will someday be like[i] the heavenly man.

[50]   What I am saying, dear brothers and sisters, is that our physical bodies cannot inherit the Kingdom of God. These dying bodies cannot inherit what will last forever.

[51]   But let me reveal to you a wonderful secret. We will not all die, but we will all be transformed! [52] It will happen in a moment, in the blink of an eye, when the last trumpet is blown. For when the trumpet sounds, those who have died will be raised to live forever. And we who are living will also be transformed. [53] For our dying bodies must be transformed into bodies that will never die; our mortal bodies must be transformed into immortal bodies. The Apostles and Prophets speaking unto you secrets and mysteries about things unheard of and hard to comprehend.

Resurrection in Hebrew means, moral aspect of redefining or recovery of spiritual truth, you cannot have a resurrection without a recovery of your own mindsets through revelation of his word and understand it when your being circumcised then you will understand. Sown in Greek Speiro means metaphorically a proverbial saying, same as a parable of the word of God. When you understand the Parables and secrets and mysteries, you will receive a resurrection immortal body back into once was the Garden of Eden.

Raise in Greek and Hebrew means to awaken from sleep from a spiritual death, some of you have the wrong inadequate testimonies and false doctrine teachings and fillings. Malachi 3: 1 Behold, I will send my messenger, and he shall prepare the way before me: and the LORD, whom ye seek, shall suddenly come to his temple, even the messenger of the covenant, whom ye delight in: behold, he shall come, saith the LORD of hosts. Suddenly in ancient Hebrew suddenly and instantly, opening of the eye in a moment, in a wink of time.
3 And he shall sit as a refiner and purifier of silver: and he shall purify the sons of Levi, and purge them as gold and silver, that they may offer unto the LORD an offering in righteousness. When you become a good offering you go up in smoke a sweet smelling fragrance unto his nostrils.

Isaiah 58:1 "Cry aloud, spare not; lift up thy voice like a trumpet! And show My people their transgression and the house of Jacob their sins. 2 Yet they seek Me daily and delight to know My ways, as a nation that did righteousness and forsook not the ordinance of their God. They ask of Me the ordinances of justice; they take delight in approaching to God.

3 'Why have we fasted,' say they, 'and Thou seest not? Why have we afflicted our soul, and thou takest no note?'

4

Behold, in the day of your fast ye find pleasure, and exact all your labors.4 Behold, ye fast for strife and debate, and to smite with the fist of wickedness; ye shall not fast as ye do this day, to make your voice to be heard on high.

5 Is it such a fast that I have chosen? A day for a man to afflict his soul? Is it to bow down his head as a bulrush, and to spread sackcloth and ashes under him? Wilt thou call this a fast, and an acceptable day to the LORD? 6 "Is not this the fast that I have chosen: to loose the bands of wickedness, to undo the heavy burdens, and to let the oppressed go free, and that ye break every yoke?

7 Is it not to deal thy bread to the hungry, and that thou bring the poor that are cast out to thy house?— when thou seest the naked, that thou cover him, and that thou hide not thyself from thine own flesh? 8 Then shall thy light break forth as the morning, and thine health shall spring forth speedily; and thy righteousness shall go before thee; the glory of the LORD shall be thy rearward. If you need healing in your body it specifically states to go and feed the poor, and help and aid those that have been cast out of shelter. When you see the are naked with no food or clothing aid them (Everything shall come to you speedily. The religious system teaches you witchcraft and opposite rituals like Tithe to the Church Sow your Seed of Money, Fast for yourself.

9 Then shalt thou call, and the LORD shall answer; thou shalt cry, and He shall say, 'Here I am.' If thou take away from the midst of thee the yoke, the putting forth of the finger and speaking vanity,10 and if thou draw out thy soul to the hungry and satisfy the afflicted soul, then shall thy light rise in obscurity (Hard times-Misery) and thy darkness be as the noonday.11 And the LORD shall guide thee continually, and satisfy thy soul in drought(Famine),

and make fat thy bones; and thou shalt be like a watered garden, and like a spring of water whose waters fail not. Fat in Hebrew cheleb, richest choice part, the marrow, Bones in Hebrew esteem, life and strength.

12 And they that shall be of thee shall build the old waste places; thou shalt raise up the foundations of many generations, and thou shalt be called the Repairer of the Breach, the Restorer of Paths to dwell in.13 "If thou turn away thy foot from the Sabbath, from doing thy pleasure on My holy day, and call the Sabbath a delight, the holy of the LORD, honorable, and shalt honor Him, not doing thine own ways, nor finding thine own pleasure, nor speaking thine own words,14 then shalt thou delight thyself in the LORD; and I will cause thee to ride upon the high places of the earth, and feed thee with the heritage of Jacob thy father; for the mouth of the LORD hath spoken it.

Sabbath is Yeshua inside you, doing his will, not thine own will, He will cause you to ride upon the high places of the earth (Increase and Favor), and feed thee the Heritage of Jacob, for Yahweh has spoken it. His Promises of richness in all things shall come to you. Saints there are False teachers everywhere, Isaiah chap 59:3 For your hands are defiled with blood, and your fingers with iniquity; your lips have spoken lies, your tongue hath muttered perverseness.4 None calleth for justice, nor any pleadeth for truth; they trust in vanity, and speak lies; they conceive mischief and bring forth iniquity. 5 They hatch adders' eggs and weave the spider's web; he that eateth of their eggs dieth, and that which is crushed breaketh out into a viper.6 Their webs shall not become garments, neither shall they cover themselves with their works; their works are works of iniquity, and the act of violence is in their hands.

These false Antichrist teachers know how to shoot spider webs at you in the spirit and attach them to your robes, Heart, mind, body, soul and spirit. Web in Hebrew or spider akkabish, to be entangled, weaving a network of systems inside you.

Until you do what they say and believe everything they tell you cunningly, using many different spirits, such also as a camellia spirit transforming different colors, using different webbed potions. To real you in and entangle you as much as possible, then when the time is ready to bite you with their fangs and place the Poison inside you for self-control over you and your household. Genesis 1:1 In the beginning God created the heaven and the earth. Create in Ancient lexicon Hebrew (Barah) means to fill or fatten. So when you receive their bites what are they filling you up with an uncreated form. Filling you up with a False genetic Counterfeit form of the Word of Eyeh Asher Eyeh.

Jeremiah 23:10 For the land is full of adulterers; for because of cursing the land mourneth; the pleasant places of the wilderness are dried up, and their course is evil, and their force is not right.11 "For both prophet and priest are profane; yea, in My house have I found their wickedness," saith the
LORD.12 "Therefore their way shall be unto them as slippery ways in the darkness; they shall be driven on, and fall therein; for I will bring evil upon them, even the year of their visitation," saith the LORD.

Now you notice is states Adulterers meaning Spiritual Adultery cheating, False teachings Saints. 13 "And I have seen folly in the prophets of Samaria: They prophesied in

Baal and caused My people Israel to err.14 I have seen also in the prophets of Jerusalem a horrible thing: They commit adultery and walk in lies; they strengthen also the hands of evildoers, that none doth return from his wickedness. They are all of them unto Me as Sodom, and the inhabitants thereof as Gomorrah ."They speak lies, Jezebel in Greek is My father is Baal, Samarian spirit, they did not follow Eyeh Asher Eyeh, it looks like God sounds like God but it is not Eyeh Asher Eyeh.

Saints remember Yeshua meets with a Samaritan woman John 4: 5 Then came He to a city of Samaria, which is called Sychar, near to the parcel of ground that Jacob gave to his son Joseph. Sychar in Hebrew means Idolatry worship of false Idols and teachings. Habakkuk 2:18 What profiteth the graven image that the maker thereof hath graven it; the molten image, and a teacher of lies, that the maker of his work trusteth therein, to make dumb idols?

John 4:9 Then said the woman of Samaria unto Him, "How is it that thou, being a Jew, askest a drink of me, who am a woman of Samaria?" For the Jews have no dealings with the Samaritans.10 Jesus answered and said unto her, "If thou knewest the gift of God and who it is that saith to thee, 'Give Me to drink,' thou would est have asked of Him, and He would have given thee living water."11 The woman said unto Him, "Sir, thou hast nothing to draw with, and the well is deep. From whence then hast thou that living water? The teaching of her Forefathers is deep within her, what well of living waters you speak of. Notice the well within her is deep rooted, but nothing to bring out.

13   Jesus answered and said unto her, "Whosoever drinketh of this water shall thirst again, your water from your ancestors are dead with no life and you continue to

thirst for truth in your inner being, 14 but whosoever drinketh of the water that I shall give him shall never thirst; but the water that I shall give him shall be in him a well of water springing up into everlasting life." 15 The woman said unto Him, "Sir, give me this water, that I thirst not, neither come hither to draw." Sir give me this understanding so that I may not thirst again. 16 Jesus said unto her, "Go, call thy husband, and come hither." Husband in Greek means-Virtue and maturity, 1 Corinthians 13:11 When I was a child, I spake as a child, I understood as a child, I thought as a child: but when I became a man, I put away childish things. Yeshua was asking her bring your teacher here. John 4: 17 The woman answered and said, "I have no husband." Jesus said unto her, "Thou hast well said, 'I have no husband';18 for thou hast had five husbands, and he whom thou now hast is not thy husband. In that thou saidst truly."

This symbolic meaning states you have deep rooted generations of filth, administering to you false teachings, meaning the generations within here go deep. Exodus 20:Thou shalt not bow down thyself to them, nor serve them: for I the LORD thy God *am* a jealous God, visiting the iniquity of the fathers upon the children unto the third and fourth *generation* of them that hate me. John 4:19 The woman said unto Him, "Sir, I perceive that thou art a prophet. A true Prophet can decipher the true hidden manna of the word of revelation in its correct form.22 Ye worship ye know not what; we know what we worship, for salvation is of the Jews. God is everything Yashua, Shua means Salvation in Hebrew. The mysteries and secrets are in the Ancient Lexicon Hebrew teachings of Yeshua. Not just what your reading in the word basic doctrine. 23 But the hour cometh and now is, when the true worshipers shall worship the Father in spirit and in truth; for the Father seeketh such to worship Him.24 God is a Spirit, and they that worship Him must worship Him in spirit and in truth." You can only get the hidden meaning by The Leading of The Holy Spirit Saints. That means all of you Saints that run here and there to many different services teachings etc, you have no clue what true teaching is and cannot discern what kind of water your drinking and food your eating. Jeremiah 23:15 Therefore thus saith the LORD of hosts concerning the prophets: "Behold, I will feed them with wormwood(Poison to Curse), and make them drink the water of gall(Poison Hemlock); for from the prophets of Jerusalem is profaneness gone forth into all the land."

Malachi 2:"And now, O ye priests, this commandment is for you. The teachers of the Torah,2 If ye will not hear, and if ye will not lay it to heart to give glory unto My name," saith the LORD of hosts, "I will even send a curse upon you, and I will curse your blessings. Yea, I have cursed them already, because ye do not lay it to heart.3 Behold, I will corrupt your seed and spread dung upon your faces, even the dung of your solemn feasts; and one shall take you away with it. The Name of Eyeh Asher Eyeh and Yeshua he speaks of Saints.

6 The law of truth was in his mouth, and iniquity was not found on his lips. He walked with Me in peace and equity, and turned many away from iniquity.7 For the priest's lips should keep knowledge, and they should seek the law at his mouth; for he is the messenger of the LORD of hosts.

They shall seek truth from Yaweh and eat and seek him Face to Face. 8 But ye have departed from the way; ye have caused many to stumble at the law(False Teachings in error); ye have corrupted the covenant of Levi," saith the LORD of hosts.9 "Therefore have I also made you contemptible and base before all the people, according as ye have not kept My ways but have been partial in the law." The father made them Despicable and bitter taste which is foul.

Malachi 3:8 Will a man rob God? Yet ye have robbed Me! But ye say, 'Wherein have we robbed Thee?' In tithes and offerings.9 Ye are cursed with a curse; for ye have robbed Me, even this whole nation. Tithe means Portion of a whole, complete reverence, the revelation of this mystery also resides in my Third book, it just stated the priests were partial in giving the law of truth, they twisted it. So when they taught and sowed seeds of manna(What kind of Meat was feed to them) within Gods Children and sent them back to me as an offering to him, they were a stench to his nostrils. Eyeh Asher Eyeh gives Shepherds to feed and nurture and instill the Character and Conduct of Yeshua, Jesus Christ. Paul the Apostle says I feed you Milk and not Solid Meat. Paul was a teacher of the Torah of truth.

Isaiah 66:20 And they shall bring all your brethren for an offering unto the LORD out of all nations upon horses, and in chariots, and in litters, and upon mules, and upon swift beasts, to my holy mountain Jerusalem, saith the LORD, as the children of Israel bring an offering in a clean vessel into the house of the LORD.21 And I will also take of them for priests and for Levites, saith the LORD.

Malachi 3 "Behold, I will send My messenger, and he shall prepare the way before Me. And the LORD, whom you seek, shall suddenly come to His temple, even the Messenger of the covenant, whom ye delight in. Behold, He shall come," saith the LORD of hosts.2 "But who may abide the day of His coming? And who shall stand when He appeareth? For He is like a refiner's fire and like fullers' soap.3 And He shall sit as a refiner and purifier of silver; and He shall purify the sons of Levi, and purge them as gold and silver, that they may offer unto the LORD an offering in righteousness. He shall bring them back unto me in character and conduct, purity, virtue, spirit and in truth. Woe to the Dictators, who pretend to be Teachers of the Mosaic law, for they have no clue what they speak of.

Woe to the False prophets and Witches and Warlock Spirit who preach Tithe and Offering is Money. Telling you, if you don't give 10 percent of your money and Offering of Money your cursed. Matthew 23:2 The scribes and Pharisees sit on Moses' seat [of authority].3 So observe and practice all they tell you; but do not do what they do, for they preach, but do not practice.4 They tie up heavy loads, hard to bear, and place them on men's shoulders, but they themselves will not lift a finger to help bear them.5 They do all their works to be seen of men; for they make wide their phylacteries ([a]small cases enclosing certain Scripture passages(They make huge warning signs and twist certain passages to their own gain), worn during prayer on the left arm and forehead) and make long their fringes [worn by all male Israelites, according to the command].

6 And they [b] take pleasure in *and* [thus] love the place of honor at feasts and the best seats in the synagogues,7 And to be greeted with honor in the marketplaces and to

have people call them rabbi. There church has become a marketing building. 13 But woe to you, scribes and Pharisees, pretenders

(hypocrites)! For you shut the kingdom of heaven in men's faces; for you neither enter yourselves, nor do you allow those who are about to go in to do so.14 [e]*Woe to you, scribes and Pharisees, pretenders (hypocrites)! For you swallow up widows' houses and for a pretense to cover it up make long prayers; therefore you will receive the greater condemnation and the heavier sentence.*

You take and twist the teachings of a widows might, the widows House in Hebrew means (treasures) telling everyone give up everything you have and cover it up with your long prayers. Telling you to give your Best and your all about and with Money. 15 Woe to you, scribes and Pharisees, pretenders (hypocrites)! For you travel over sea and land to make a single proselyte, and when he becomes one [a proselyte], you make him doubly as much a child of hell (Gehenna) as you are. 25 Woe to you, scribes and Pharisees, pretenders (hypocrites)! For you clean the outside of the cup and of the plate, but within they are full of extortion (prey, spoil, plunder) and grasping self-indulgence. Extortion-the practice of obtaining something, especially money. The Practice of false teaching of money storytelling, making huge cases on money scriptures and demands of fear warnings signs if you do not Tithe and Offering with your money your cursed. The Scripture in the bible says to give what you have made a decision in your heart without grudgingly. 26 You blind Pharisee! First clean the inside of the cup and of the plate, so that the outside may be clean also.27 Woe to you, scribes and Pharisees, pretenders (hypocrites)! For you are like tombs that have been whitewashed, which look beautiful on the outside but inside are full of dead men's bones and everything impure.28 Just so, you also outwardly seem to people to be just *and* upright but inside you are full of pretense and lawlessness *and* iniquity.29 Woe to you, scribes and Pharisees, pretenders (hypocrites)! For you build tombs for the prophets and decorate the monuments of the righteous.

Lamentations 3:15 He hath filled me with bitterness; He hath made me drunken with wormwood.16 He hath also broken my teeth with gravel stones; He hath covered me with ashes.17 And Thou hast removed my soul far off from peace; I forgot prosperity.18 And I said, "My strength and my hope are perished from the LORD,"Wormwood is Poison bitterness, Hemlock in Hebrew.

Amos 5:6 Seek the LORD, and ye shall live; lest He break out like fire in the house of Joseph, and devour it, and there be none to quench it in Bethel—7 ye who turn judgment to wormwood, and leave off righteousness in the earth! "Poison false teachings, wormwood, false prophecies. Amos 6:11 For behold, the LORD commandeth, and He will smite the great house with breaches, and the little house with clefts.12 Shall horses run upon the rock? Will one plow there with oxen? For ye have turned judgment into gall, and the fruit of righteousness into hemlock. Twisted teachings into poison.

Saints watch this Revelation 8:10 And the third angel sounded, and there fell a great star from heaven, burning as if it were a lamp, and it fell upon a third part of the rivers and upon the fountains of waters;11 and the name of the star is called Wormwood. And a third part of the waters became wormwood; and many men died from the waters, because they were made bitter. Star someone that has a great name or audience, big ministry, TV Land, their own Show, Network on TV. Water is the Multitudes of peoples and nations he is speaking of.

Watch carefully saints Jude 1:4 For certain men have crept in stealthily [[c]gaining entrance secretly by a side door]. Their doom was predicted long ago, ungodly (impious, profane) persons who pervert the grace (the spiritual blessing and favor) of our God into lawlessness *and* wantonness *and* immorality, and disown *and* deny our sole Master and Lord, Jesus Christ (the Messiah, the Anointed One).

7 [The wicked are sentenced to suffer] just as Sodom and Gomorrah and the adjacent towns—which likewise gave themselves over to impurity and indulged in unnatural vice *and* sensual perversity—are laid out [in plain sight] as an exhibit of perpetual punishment [to warn] of everlasting fire.8 Nevertheless in like manner, these dreamers also corrupt the body, scorn *and* reject authority *and* government, and revile *and* libel *and* scoff at [heavenly] glories (the glorious ones).

10 But these men revile (scoff and sneer at) anything they do not happen to be acquainted with *and* do not understand; and whatever they do understand physically [that which they know by mere instinct], like irrational beasts—by these they corrupt themselves *and* are destroyed (perish).

11 Woe to them! For they have run riotously in the way of Cain, and have abandoned themselves for the sake of gain [it offers them, following] the error of Balaam, and have perished in rebellion [like that] of Korah!12 These

are hidden reefs (elements of danger) in your love feasts, where they boldly feast sumptuously [carousing together in your midst], without scruples providing for themselves [alone]. They are clouds without water, swept along by the winds; trees, without fruit at the late autumn gathering time—twice (doubly) dead, [lifeless and] plucked up by the roots;13 Wild waves of the sea, flinging up the foam of their own shame *and* disgrace; wandering stars, for whom the gloom of eternal darkness has been reserved forever.

They are wandering Stars, whom gloom of eternal Darkness has been reserved forever. Jeremiah 23:15 Therefore thus says the Lord of hosts concerning the prophets: Behold, I will feed them with [the bitterness of] wormwood and make them drink the [poisonous] water of gall, for from the [false] prophets of Jerusalem profaneness *and* ungodliness have gone forth into all the land.

16   Thus says the Lord of hosts: Do not listen to the words of the [false] prophets who prophesy to you. They teach you vanity (emptiness, falsity, and futility) *and* fill you with vain hopes; they speak a vision of their own minds and not from the mouth of the Lord.

17   They are continually saying to those who despise Me *and* the word of the Lord, The Lord has said: You shall have peace; and they say to everyone who walks after the stubbornness of his own mind *and* heart, No evil shall come upon you.

Saints just look at the word of these passages of Scripture 25 I have heard what the prophets have said who prophesy lies in My name, saying, I have dreamed, I have dreamed [visions on my bed at night].26 [How long shall this state of things continue?] How long yet shall it be in the minds of the prophets who prophesy falsehood, even the prophets of the deceit of their own hearts,27 Who think that they can cause My people to forget My name by their dreams which every man tells to his neighbor, just as their fathers forgot My name because of Baal?28 The prophet who has a dream, let him tell his dream; but he who has My word, let him speak My word faithfully. What has straw in common with wheat [for nourishment]? says the Lord.29 Is not My word like fire [that consumes all that cannot endure the test]? says the Lord, and like a hammer that breaks in pieces the rock [of most stubborn resistance]?

The Apostles and Prophets are like hammers breaking in pieces the rock of stubbornness inside or within you, remember in my recent book I spoke of the word Intrusion An **intrusion** is liquid rock that forms under Earth's surface. Magma from under the surface is slowly pushed up from deep within the earth into any cracks or spaces it can find, sometimes pushing existing country rock out of the way, a process that can take millions of years. As the rock slowly cools into a solid, the different parts of the magma crystallize into minerals.

Saints the mystery of the veils being opened, the secrets and mysteries of his Kingdom. Revelation 11:1 *The temple is commanded to be measured.   3 The Lord stirred up two witnesses,   7 whom the beast murdereth,   9 and no man burieth them.   11 God raiseth them to life,   12 and calleth them up to heaven,   13 the wicked are terrified, 15 by the trumpet of the seventh Angel the resurrection, 18 and judgment is described.*

1   [a]Then was given me a reed like unto a rod, and the Angel stood by, saying, Rise and [b]mete the Temple of

God, and the Altar, and them that worship therein. We shall be Measured,(Numbers 17:And the LORD said unto Moses, Bring Aaron's rod again before the testimony(Ark of the Covenant), to be kept for a token against the rebels; and thou shalt quite take away their murmurings from me, that they die not. Revelation 2:27 AND HE SHALL RULE THEM WITH A ROD OF IRON, AS THE VESSELS OF THE POTTER ARE BROKEN TO PIECES, as I also have received authority from My Father;

2   [c]But the [d]Court which is without the Temple(Without the Holy Spirit or the Immature) [e]cast out, and mete it not: for it is given unto the [f]Gentiles, and the holy city shall they tread under foot, [g]two and forty Months. 3 ½ years, the outer court 1500 cubits, the time when Moses met the angel of Eyey Asher Eyeh, the inner court (Church age) 10x20x10=2,000. Treading out the grain since Yeshua birth and Resurrection until now. Total is 3,500 years all together.

3   But [h]I will give power unto my two witnesses and they shall [i]prophesy a thousand two hundred and threescore days, clothed in sackcloth. 1,290 days a Transfiguration is about to take place 1+2+9+12 add the o at the end 120, it took Noah 120years to build the Ark. There was a Transfiguration taking place of a New age and a New World at hand. The last 3,500 years the spirit of Prophecy and thy Testimonies have lived on.

4   These [j]are two olive trees, and two candlesticks, standing before the God of the earth. Zechariah 4:2 And said unto me, What seest thou? And I said, I have looked, and behold, a [a]candlestick all of gold with a bowl upon the top of it, and his seven lamps therein, and seven [b]pipes to the lamps which were upon the top thereof,3

And two olive trees over it, one upon the right side of the bowl, and the other upon the left side thereof.

6 Then he answered and spake unto me, saying, This is the word of the Lord unto [c]Zerubbabel, saying, Neither by [d]an army nor strength, but by my Spirit, saith the Lord of hosts. 10 For who hath despised the day of the [h]small things? but they shall rejoice, and shall see the stone of [i]tin in the hand of Zerubbabel: [j]these seven are the eyes of the Lord, which go through the whole world. The seven spirits of Eyeh Asher Eyeh, 12 And I spake moreover, and said unto him, What be these two olive branches, which through the two golden pipes empty themselves into the gold? Those purified by fire and death to self and circumcised thine hearts unto me.

14 Then said he, These are the two [k]olive branches, that stand with the ruler of the whole earth. Yeshua is the Ruler of the Whole earth. Revelation 11:5 [k]And if any man will hurt them, fire proceedeth out of their mouths and devoureth their enemies: for if any man would hurt them, thus must he be killed. Not speaking of a natural death but of a Spiritual death.

Revelation 11:6 These have power to shut heaven, that it rain not in the days of their prophesying, and have power over waters to turn them into blood, and to smite the earth with all manner plagues, as often as they will. The spirit of Elijah and Moses symbolically. Dominion and Authority of his Spirit.

7   [l]And when they have [m]finished their testimony, [n]the beast that cometh out of the bottomless pit, shall make war against them, and shall [o]overcome them, and kill them. Revelation 13:5 And there was given unto him a mouth speaking great things and blasphemies; and power

was given unto him to continue forty *and* two months. To kill also means to try to shut up or stop the mouth or prophecies(3,500years).

8   And their corpses shall lie in the [p]streets of the great city, which [q]spiritually is called Sodom and
Egypt, [r]where our Lord also was crucified. Spiritually speaking the inner man was of Sodom and Egypt, Sodom in Hebrew Sedom-Dead sea, corrupt sin, Egypt means Double minded and a Double Tongue. We have been Crucifying Yeshua inside of us with our old Nature.

9   And they of the people and kindred's, and tongues, and Gentiles, shall see their corpses [s]three days and an half Corpse(Dead things, idolatry teachings), and shall not suffer their carcasses to be put in graves(putting the people in graves in there spirit inner man).

10   And they that dwell upon the earth, [t]shall rejoice over them and be glad, and shall send gifts one to another, for these two Prophets [u]vexed them that dwelt on the earth. The false prophets which had Dead things in them Corrupt teachings and Idolatry in them, also having a Double tongues.

11   [v]But after [w]three days and an half, [x]the spirit of life *coming* from God, shall enter into them, and they [y]shall stand up upon their feet: and great fear shall come upon them which saw them. After 3,500 years the spirit of life of Eyeh Asher Eyeh shall enter in them, like a moment in a twinkling of an eye.

12   And they shall hear a great voice from heaven, saying unto them, [z]Come up hither: And they shall ascend up to heaven in a cloud, [aa]and their enemies shall see them. Isaiah 40: It is he who sits above the circle of the earth,

and its inhabitants are like grasshoppers;who stretches out the heavens like a curtain,and spreads them like a tent to dwell in. Ascending in our Consciousness transformed into a greater understanding of Spirit realm and also natural Immortal Bodies.

13 [ab]And the same hour shall there be a great earthquake(Awakening), and the tenth part of the city shall fall(His Remnant), and in the earthquake shall be slain(Raptured in Spirit,Slain Transformed in Spirit and Naturally) in number seven thousand(Perfection): and the remnant were sore feared, [ac]and [ad]gave glory to God of heaven. A great earthquake meaning an Awakening, his remnant which have became or have become into Perfection and Gave Glory to Eyeh Asher Eyeh.

14 [ae]The second woe is past, *and* behold, the third woe will come anon. Anon in Arabic or Hebrew means Immediately. 15 [af]And the seventh Angel blew the trumpet, and there were great voices in heaven, saying, [ag]The kingdoms of the world are our Lord's, and his Christ's, and he shall reign for evermore(Resurrection) twenty Elders, which sat before God on their seats, fell upon their faces and worshiped God. The 24 resembles is in my third book, 12 tribes of Israel. Israel and 12 Foundations which had the 12 apostles names on the Foundations, the prophets of old had Authority and Dominion just like the Apostles were given authority and dominion.

17 Saying, We give thee thanks, Lord God Almighty, Which art, and which wast, and which art to come: for thou hast received thy great might, and hast obtained thy kingdom. Which art(Masterworks man), He has come (Approached us and Dwelt within us) and received thy

great might and hast obtained thy kingdom of Heaven and also Earth.

18 [ai]And the Gentiles were angry, and thy wrath is come, and the time of the dead(Those who were asleep), that they should be judged, and that thou should est give reward unto thy servants the Prophets, and to thy Saints, and to them that fear thy Name, to small and great, and should est destroy them, which destroy the earth. Judgment takes place for the earth through His wisdom.

19 Then the Temple of God was [aj]opened in heaven(Immortal body dwelt within man), and there was seen in the Temple the Ark of his covenant(We were placed in the Ark Holy of Holies) and there were lightnings (Hebrew means Barak, Flaming Sword glittering), and voices(Rejoicing), and thundering s(Stir of the Spirit), and earthquake(Awakening), and much hail(Revelations and Mysteries and Secrets for 1,000 years. My mother was prophesied that when she gets to heaven she will have vaults and libraries of books for herself, this means symbolically Eyeh Asher Eyeh will give her the Libraries here and Now when we transform into our Immortal bodies. She is going to own Libraries filled with myriads of Revelations and Secrets and Mysteries.

Romans 6:5 For if we have become united with him in the likeness of his death, we shall be also in the likeness of his resurrection. His exact transfiguration form Saints. Saints let's move on, Psalms 97: The LORD reigneth, let the earth rejoice! Let the multitude of isles be glad thereof!2 Clouds and darkness are round about Him; righteousness and judgment are the habitation of His throne. Cloud In Hebrew means witness we are his witnesses,3 A fire goeth before Him(Fire in Hebrew Means anger, pressed or despair meaning Pressure, Paul says I Glory in my

Tribulations), and burneth up His enemies round about. He is Saying Burning out the wood hay and stubble within us, we are our own enemy.4 His lightnings enlightened the world; the earth saw and trembled.5 The hills melted like wax at the presence of the LORD, at the presence of the Lord of the whole earth.6 The heavens declare His righteousness(Right understanding), and all the people see His glory. The word Burned up, Hebrew Lahat Flaming sword in Genesis Covering the Garden of Eden. Burning means to cover a veil or secret in Ancient Hebrew lexicon, Tet Lamed, a cover to hide what is behind. The fire of Ayeh Asher Ayeh is the secrets of the Garden of the church going back into the Glory.

Zechariah 14:4 And his feet shall stand in that day upon the mount of Olives, which *is* before Jerusalem on the east, and the mount of Olives shall cleave in the midst thereof toward the east and toward the west, *and there shall be* a very great valley; and half of the mountain shall remove toward the north, and half of it toward the south. Mountain in Hebrew Har, summoned to praise or High place and promotion, Olive in Hebrew Zayit represents His oil of Anointing, This symbolic meaning we shall be put to the test from left to right, we shall grow and mature, some will come up hither unto him and some will fall away from him. Then it states Half the Mountain shall remove toward the North and go into the Holy of Holies of Transformation and some shall move toward the South the outer Court.

Mountain also means the Mind, Matthew 17:And Yehsua said unto them, Because of your unbelief: for verily I say unto you, If ye have faith as a grain of mustard seed(A little small mustard seed of Revelation), ye shall say unto this mountain(Mind0, Remove hence to yonder place; and it shall remove; and nothing shall be impossible unto you.

It means and he is SAYING it will remove a Mountain of Carnality.

Light in Hebrew ancient lexicon means Order or box, Light also means necessary for order. Boxes are used to keep things in order. So when you receive the light you receive order, 1 Corinthians 14:40 Let all things be done decently and in order. Paul was talking about understanding the Revelation of Ayeh Asher Ayeh.

Psalms 97:The LORD reigneth, let the earth rejoice! Let the multitude of isles be glad thereof!2 Clouds and darkness are round about Him; righteousness and judgment are the habitation of His throne.3 A fire goeth before Him, and burneth up His enemies roundabout.4 His lightnings enlightened the world; the earth saw and trembled. Saints Clouds resemble witnesses us, Darkness is the hidden riches of his secret mysteries. Lightning in Hebrew Barah, also means flaming sword, Eyeh's flaming sword flashes with Power of His Spirit and word.

CHAPTER 2

Psalms 97: 7 Confounded be all they that serve graven images, that boast themselves of idols. Worship Him, all ye gods! 8 Zion heard and was glad, and the daughters of Judah rejoiced because of Thy judgments, O LORD.9 For Thou, LORD, art high above all the earth; Thou art exalted far above all gods.10 Ye that love the LORD, hate evil! He preserveth the souls of His saints; He delivereth them out of the hand of the wicked.11 Light is sown for the righteous, and gladness for the upright in heart.12 Rejoice in the LORD, ye righteous, and give thanks at the remembrance of His holiness. Seed and Sown in Hebrew means Zarah, Semen, Ayeh is impregnating us with light, and trying to get us Pregnant with his Revelation to give birth to his Nature!.

Joel 2:2 Blow ye the trumpet in Zion, and sound an alarm in My holy mountain! Let all the inhabitants of the land tremble; for the day of the LORD cometh, for it is nigh at hand—2 a day of darkness and of gloominess, a day of clouds and of thick darkness, as the morning spread upon the mountains. A great people and a strong, there hath not been ever the like; neither shall be any more after it, even to the years of many generations. It specifically states there has never ever been like this army, even to the years of many generations 1,000 years. 3 A fire devoureth before them, and behind them a flame burneth. The land is as the Garden of Eden before them, and behind them a desolate wilderness; yea, and nothing shall escape them. The land before them is like the Garden of Eden, Which is also speaking as us.

Daniel 9:24 This is the Seventy (Sevens) "Seventy weeks are determined concerning thy people and concerning thy holy city to finish the transgression and to make an end of sins, and to make reconciliation for iniquity, and to bring in everlasting righteousness, and to seal up the vision and prophecy, and to anoint the Most Holy. The 7 weeks by 70 symbol(7), 7x7 equals 49, there are saying according to the Rabbis, there are taking 49 weeks multiplying by 360 days which is according to the

Hebrew Calendar. It comes out to 17,460 days. Ultimately, the only time, and truly as I see it, the ONLY time you can apply the 7 weeks of Daniel, which start from the going forth of the command to restore and build Jerusalem, is when you use June 7, 1967 as a starting point...and you end up 17460 days later at the feast Atonement Sept 23, 2015. It all fits logically, perfectly, and structurally.

25   Know therefore and understand that from the going forth of the commandment to restore and to build Jerusalem until the Messiah the Prince, shall be seven weeks and threescore and two weeks; the street shall be built again, and the wall, even in troublesome times. The seven weeks (7) and two weeks 7days in one week (7)(7), symbolically 7x7 equals 49 times 360 days equals 17,460 days. The Three score also symbolically means 30 day months according to Hebrew Calendar.

26   And after threescore and two weeks shall Messiah be cut off, but not for Himself; and the people of the prince who shall come shall destroy the city and the sanctuary. And the end thereof shall be with a flood, and until the end of the war desolation's are determined. Symbolically score means (20) also, threescore is 60 and two weeks equals 62x7 equals 434 years. Furthermore from 1535 Suleiman the Magnificent rebuilt Jerusalem. Saints 1535

plus 434 Equals 1969 two years after 1967 of the decree of Jerusalem to be rebuilt a love letter was written by Stanley Gold foot (The Times of Israel). This symbolism will be understand more several paragraphs below, 483 years minus 434 equals 49.

27   And he shall confirm the covenant with many for one week; and in the midst of the week he shall cause the sacrifice and the oblation to cease. And for the overspreading of abominations he shall make it desolate, even until the consummation, and that determined shall be poured upon the desolate. "Then it states he shall confirm the covenant for one week (7) perfection is near.

God at Jerusalem, Let the house be builded, the place where they offered sacrifices, and let the the breadth thereof threescore cubits; Ezra 6:3 (circa 457 B.C.)

Know therefore and understand, [that] from the going forth of the commandment to restore and to build Jerusalem unto the Messiah the Prince [shall be] seven weeks, and threescore and two weeks: the street shall be built again, and the wall, even in troublous times. Dan.9 :25,69 x 7 sabbatical weeks =483 yrs.

In this time of understanding Persian Artaxerxes Longimnus who issued the decree to restore and rebuild Jerusalem in 445 BC (Nehemiah 2). On the 483rd Anniversary of this decree Yeshua rode into Jerusalem on a Donkey on what we know as the First Palm Sunday, fulfilling the Prophecy of Daniel 9:25. Then in 68-70Ad the city was destroyed by the Romans. After centuries of being rebuilt and then torn down by various conquering groups, the walls around Jerusalem were finally rebuilt under the direction of Suleiman the Magnificent beginning in 1535 AD, and during his reign the city enjoyed an exceptional period of peace and religious tolerance. Saints for the most part, these are the walls that surround the Old City today.

Based on my understanding of Matt 24:34 and Psalm 90:10 Yeshua the Tabernacle age or Kingdom age Should commence in 2018, 70years after the re-birth of Israel. If so it will have been 483 years since Suleiman ordered Jerusalem's walls rebuilt, the same span of time given in Daniel 9:25.In 1948 Israel was a free nation 70 years plus 1948 equals 2018. 1535–1538:

Suleiman the Magnificent rebuilds walls around Jerusalem. Inside Wikipedia link. The **Walls of Jerusalem** (Arabic: أسوار القدس; Hebrew: חומות ירושלים) surround the old city of Jerusalem (approx. 1 km²). The walls were built between 1535 and 1538, when Jerusalem was part of the Ottoman Empire, by the order of Suleiman I.

Ephesians 3:9 and to make all men see what is the fellowship of the mystery, which from the beginning of the world hath been hid in God, who created all things by Jesus Christ, 10 with the intent that now unto the principalities and powers in heavenly places might be known through the church the manifold wisdom of God. The word Great in Hebrew Root means Head of the Family, men with divine wisdom, also goes on to say strength, archer shooting arrows, to go deep into his mystery. We are called to show the Principalities of Eyeh's Glory. Fallen means to be fallen from the truth, the church is under control of the Fallen angels the Nephilim's religious systems. Wicked in Hebrew means one who has departed or walked away from the Path.

Isaiah 60:4 "Lift up thine eyes round about and see; all they gather themselves together, they come to thee; thy sons shall come from far, and thy daughters shall be nursed at thy side.5 Then thou shalt see and flow together, and thine heart shall fear and be enlarged, because the abundance of the sea shall be converted unto thee (Infinite Knowledge of Revelation shall be downloaded within), the wealth of the Gentiles shall come unto thee.

6 The multitude of camels shall cover thee, the dromedaries of Median and Ephah; all they from Sheba shall come; they shall bring gold and incense, and they shall show forth the praises of the LORD.7 All the flocks of Kedar shall be gathered together unto thee, the rams of Nebaioth shall minister unto thee; they shall come up with acceptance on Mine altar, and I will glorify the house of My glory.

8 "Who are these that fly as a cloud and as the doves to their windows?9 Surely the isles shall wait for Me—and the ships of Tarshish first, to bring thy sons from far, their silver and their gold with them, unto the name of the LORD thy God, and to the Holy One of Israel, because He hath glorified thee. Who are these that carry the Presence of his Shekinah Glory, as the Doves the Holy spirit and can see all things.

10 "And the sons of strangers shall build up thy walls, and their kings shall minister unto thee; for in My wrath I smote thee, but in My favor have I had mercy on thee.11 Therefore thy gates shall be open continually; they shall not be shut day nor night, that men may bring unto thee the wealth of the Gentiles, and that their kings may be

brought. Those within have the Portal and keys to heaven and is open 24/7.

13 The glory of Lebanon shall come unto thee, the fir tree, the pine tree, and the box together to beautify the place of My sanctuary; and I will make the place of My feet glorious. 15 "Whereas thou hast been forsaken and hated, so that no man went through thee, I will make thee an eternal excellency, a joy of many generations. Notice it says eternal excellency joy of many generations. External means outside the body.

16 Thou shalt also suck the milk of the Gentiles, and shalt suck the breast of kings; and thou shalt know that I the LORD, am thy Savior and thy Redeemer, the mighty One of Jacob.17 "For brass I will bring gold, and for iron I will bring silver, and for wood, brass, and for stones, iron. I will also make thy officers peace and thine ex actors righteousness. Removing the milk of understanding within the Gentiles and the Kings and give them proper food, turning into purified silver and gold. Wood is unrighteousness, Brass is lukewarmness, stone regular sound doctrine no revelation, iron denial, Pride.

18 Violence shall no more be heard in thy land, wasting nor destruction within thy borders; but thou shalt call thy walls Salvation and thy gates Praise.21 Thy people also shall be all righteous; they shall inherit the land for ever, the branch of My planting, the work of My hands, that I may be glorified. 22 A little one shall become a thousand, and a small one a strong nation; I, the LORD, will hasten it in his time." A little shall live a Thousand Years.

Isaiah 65:8 Thus saith the LORD, "As the new wine is found in the cluster, and one saith, 'Destroy it not, for a blessing is in it,' so will I do for my servants' sakes, that I may not destroy them all.9 And I will bring forth a seed out of Jacob, and out of Judah an inheritor of My mountains; and Mine elect shall inherit it, and My servants shall dwell there.10 And Sharon shall be a fold of flocks, and the Valley of Achor a place for the herds to lie down in, for My people that have sought Me. Cluster in Greek botrus: a cluster of grapes, the vine the root that is hidden within Yeshua.

Isaiah 65:17 "For, behold, I create new heavens and a new earth; and the former shall not be remembered, nor come into mind.18 But be ye glad and rejoice for ever in that which I create; for behold, I create Jerusalem a rejoicing, and her people a joy.19 And I will rejoice in Jerusalem, and joy in My people; and the voice of weeping shall be no more heard in her, nor the voice of crying.

20 There shall be no more thence an infant of days, nor an old man that hath not filled his days; for the child shall die a hundred years old; but the sinner being a hundred years old shall be accursed.21 And they shall build houses and inhabit them; and they shall plant vineyards and eat the fruit of them.22 They shall not build and another inhabit; they shall not plant and another eat; for as the days of a tree are the days of My people, and Mine elect shall long enjoy the work of their hands. Trees live over 1,000 years.

Saints let,s move on, In the beginning of Creation, the 1ˢᵗ day is a wheel within a wheel, Jacobs latter realm of deep levels. The circle is the Hidden meaning of the outer wheel. He is the Rest and the beginning, Alaf Tav-beginning and end, Ezekiel he speaks of Chariots Ezekiel 1: And when the living creatures went, the wheels went with them: and when the living creatures were lifted up from the earth, the wheels were lifted up. Yod-Arm, Hey means attention Teacher, Vav nail Crucifying of Self, Hey Revelation Disciple. That is why the Number 0 has a number and is a number, we have just Quantified our existence to numbers, 0 infinite. Suspened in Mid-air, Yod is the smallest of the Hebrew letters, the "Atom" of the consonants, and the Form from which all of the other letters begin and end. Vav is the Divine Order of the "Hook" of creation. Ephesians 3:18 may be able to comprehend with all saints what is the breadth and length and depth and height. The Dot is the Yod the Depth, Vav is the Length.

The Gem atriaa of the word Yod is symbolic 20 Hebrew root Vision Chazah. Now In Hebrew the meaning of Yod is Ten, we have ten fingers and ten toes which makes 20. Our eyesight we have 20/20 vision. Exodus 32:15 And Moses turned and went down from the mountain, and the two tablets of the testimony *were* in his hand, tablets written on their two sides; *on the front and on the back*[i] they were written. 16 And the tablets, they *were* the work of God; and the writing, it *was* the writing of God engraved on the tablets. Exodus 40:20 And he took and put the testimony into the ark, and set the staves on the ark, and put the mercy seat above upon the ark. The testimony was the written word Yah, Exodus 32:19 *And*[j] as he came near to the camp, he saw the bull calf and dancing, and *Moses became angry,*[k] and he threw the tablets from his hand, and he broke them under the mountain. The Testimony ascended and flew off the stone tablets and returned unto Yahweh to tell on them. The Testimony contained the weight of the stones, Moses could no longer hold them they were to heavy. The Yoke

Left and the Burden left.

Matthew 11:13 For my yoke *is* easy, and my burden is light. The Seed is The word, which is Christ. John 3:13 No one has ascended into heaven except he who descended from heaven, the Son of Man. Now let me explain the Mystery of his supreme ship within us. Psalms 18:11 He made darkness his secret place; his pavilion round about him *were* dark waters *and* thick clouds of the skies. We are the likeness his image in his shadow of his wings within us, we become his Shadow. The brightness of his light is within us and shall radiate in and through us. Hebrew 3:11 Therefore I swear in my wrath, If they shall enter into my rest. When you do normally rest at night when its dark.12 [o]Take heed brethren, lest at any time there be in any of you an evil heart, and unfaithful, to depart away from the living God. Meaning if you receive the revelation of his understanding and a circumcised heart you will fall into this rest. Meaning you will not have to lift a finger to work and be in hardship or toil the sweat of your brow in any kind of way shape or form.

Hebrews 4:2 For indeed we have had the glad tidings [Gospel of God] proclaimed to us just as truly as they [the Israelite s of old did when the good news of deliverance from bondage came to them]; but the message they heard did not benefit them, because it was not mixed with faith (with [c]the leaning of the entire personality(Gratitude) on God in absolute trust and confidence in His power, wisdom, and goodness) by those who heard it; [d] *neither were they united in faith with the ones [Joshua and Caleb] who heard (did believe).*

3   For we who have believed (adhered to and trusted in and relied on God) do enter that rest, [e]in accordance with His declaration that those [who did not believe]

should not enter when He said, As I swore in My wrath, They shall not enter My rest; and this He said although [His] works had been completed *and* prepared [and waiting for all who would believe] from the foundation of the world.

4   For in a certain place He has said this about the seventh day: And God rested on the seventh day from all His works. Infinite wisdom he speaks a mystery right here Saints.5 And [they forfeited their part in it, for] in this [passage] He said, They shall not enter My rest.

6   Seeing then that the promise remains over [from past times] for some to enter that rest, and that those who formerly were given the good news (Secrets mysteries Revelations) about it *and* the opportunity, failed to appropriate it(You did not receive it or You eat it and spit it right back out) *and* did not enter because of disobedience,

7   Again He sets a definite day, [a new] Today, [and gives another opportunity of securing that rest] saying through David after so long a time in the words already quoted, Today, if you would hear His voice *and* when you hear it, do not harden your hearts.8 [This mention of a rest was not a reference to their entering into Canaan.] For if Joshua had given them rest, He [God] would not speak afterward about another day. It specifically says your in the rest of Canaan the Tithe and rules and regulations and False teachings land.

9 So then, there is still awaiting a full *and* complete Sabbath-rest reserved for the [true] people of God;10 For he who has once entered [God's] rest also has ceased from [the weariness and pain] of human labors, just as God rested from those labors [f]peculiarly His own. Hello

Saints this mystery speaks right here.

11 Let us therefore be zealous *and* exert ourselves *and* strive diligently to enter that rest [of God, to know and experience it for ourselves], that no one may fall *or* perish by the same kind of unbelief *and* disobedience [into which those in the wilderness fell]. Let me Give you a Revelation Saints Ready, im going to give you the Twisted Teaching of the Tithe, Genesis 14:17 After his [Abram's] return from the defeat *and* slaying of Chedorlaomer and the kings who were with him, the king of Sodom went out to meet him at the Valley of Shaveh, that is, the King's Valley.

18 Melchizedek king of Salem [later called Jerusalem] brought out bread and wine [for their nourishment]; he was the priest of God Most High, (Communion they had Communion bread and wine just like the shadow of things to come Yeshua the bread of life and wine his blood)

19 And he blessed him and said, Blessed (favored with blessings, made blissful, joyful) be Abram by God Most High, Possessor *and* Maker of heaven and earth,20 And blessed, praised, *and* glorified be God Most High, who has given your foes into your hand! And [Abram] gave him a tenth of all [he had taken]. He Tithed out of the Portion from the Spoils of war from a Fight he just had and Conquered a certain City not out of his own Income. Watch this Saints,21 And the king of Sodom said to Abram, give me the persons and keep the goods for yourself. Melchizedek and King of Sodom said keep the Tithe I don't want it. They wanted the people not the tithe, You notice in many congregations today the Leaders and Teachers keep the People for themselves and never transform them into Yeshua's likeness and receive a circumcised heart, they control them to get the Tithe, they will not let go of the People.

According to the Levitical Priesthood the rules were so Strict they were not allowed to own Anything, they were not allowed to have an Inheritance at all. There focus was to be on Yah alone, Luke 14:33 (Phi) "Only the man who says goodbye to all his possessions can be my disciple." Now how does this pertain to Conquer ship mode here we go, I also spoke about the Revelation of the Two Witnesses its symbolic meaning is Conquer ship mode. Melchizedek and the King of Sodom, who were so rich and wealthy who had all things. Increase of Rest, beyond our comprehension he is speaking of, spiritually and naturally.

Now saints I'm going to give you some symbolic meaning of History and tie some Revelations together to fit into truth.

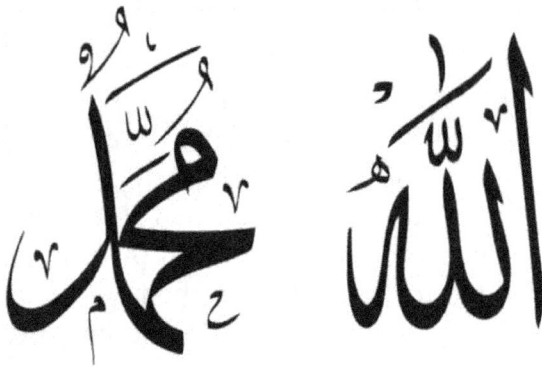

محمد الله

٣ع

6 is sigma, ς Σσς *sigma sam (s,V) 6, 200 final form

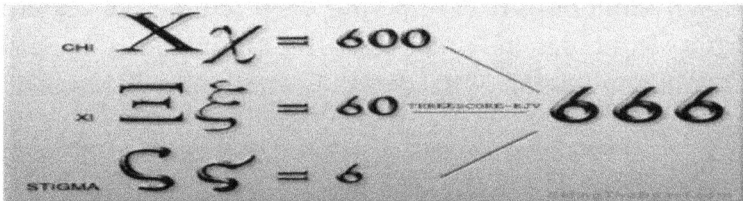

THE GREEK ALPHABET

UNITS	TENS	HUNDREDS
Stigma $\varsigma^1 = 6$	Xi $\Xi \ \xi^2 = 60$	Chi $X \ \chi = 600$

These symbolic meaning will all come into play as you read and continue your understanding for truth in the Holy Spirit and Revelations. My Heart is for truth and understanding that we all come to the end of ourselves and die to self completely and open our Hearts and ears to complete truth in all things for gain and birth the character of Yeshua within us all.

Allahu Akbar

Greek letters representing 666

These symbolic meaning are to introduce to you enlightenment of the truth where everything is originated from. The Meat of Revelation is found in the Holy Spirit, the Hidden Manna of His divine Revelation to all Mankind.

The Hindu God of Shiva Buddhism...............

According to an archaeologist glancing through research material, pleasantly surprised to come across a reference to a king Vikramaditya inscription found in Kaaba in Mecca proving beyond doubt that the Arabian Peninsula formed a part of his Indian Empire.

The text of the crucial Vikramaditya inscribed on a gold dish hung inside the Kaaba shrine of Mecca, is found recorded on Page 315 of a volume known as 'Sayar-ul-Okul' treasured in the Makhtab-e-Sultania library in Istanbul, Turkey.

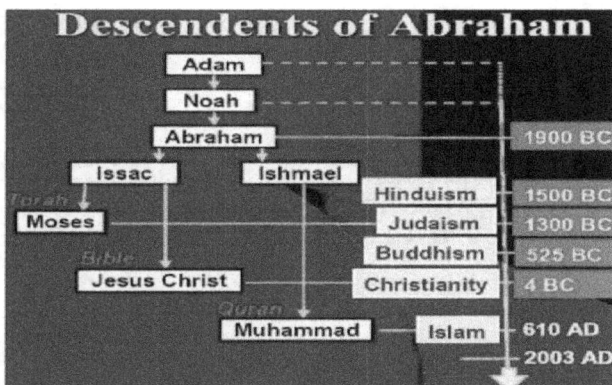

Descendents of Abraham

- Adam
- Noah
- Abraham — 1900 BC
  - Issac
  - Ishmael
    - Hinduism — 1500 BC
    - Moses — Judaism — 1300 BC
    - Buddhism — 525 BC
    - Jesus Christ — Christianity — 4 BC
    - Muhammad — Islam — 610 AD
      — 2003 AD

Torah
Bible
Quran

References About Muhammad in Hindu Scriptures

1. **Verse 5 of Bhavishya Puran:** "…His name will be Mahamad… Mahadev Arab… 'O Ye! The pride of mankind, the dweller in Arabia."… (*Prati Sarg Parv III*).

   Verse 5 of Bhavishya Puran, Prati Sarg Parv III: 3, 3:

   एत्रस्मिन्नन्तरे म्लेच्छ आचार्येण समन्विवतः ।
   His name will be Mahamad:
   महामद् इति ख्यातः शिष्यशाखासमन्वितः ॥ ५ ॥
   Bhavishya Puran: Prati Sarg, Part III: 3, 3, 5

2. **Sama Veda, II, 6, 8:** "Ahmad acquired religious law from his Lord. This law of religion is full of wisdom."

   अह्यमिधे पितुः परिषद्यामूवस्य जग्रह । अहं सूर्य इवाजनि ॥
   सामवेद० । प्र० २ । द० ६ । मं० ८ ॥

Crescent on Shiva's Head	Islam crescent
Crescent: Shiva bears on his head the crescent of the panchami (fifth day) moon. The moon is also a measure of time, thus Crescent also represent his control over time.	Per Islam crescent moon signifies the beginning of the 4 weeks of Ramadan, Islam's holiest month. It is also symbol of time. In other words used to calculate days months in calendar.

Hindu Prayer ritual	Islam Prayer ritual
"Sashtang" **Bowing in front of God with eight limbs touching the ground**	**Bowing in front of God with eight limbs touching the ground.**
	Source: "http://en.wikipedia.org/wiki/Salah"

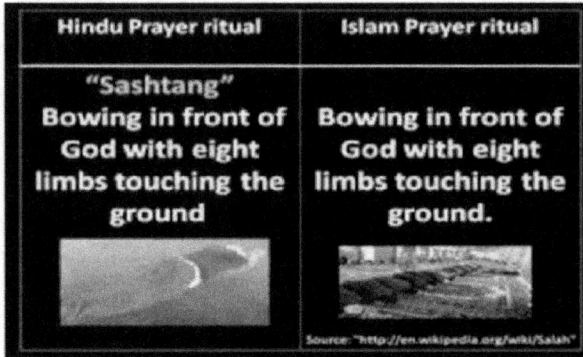

The book Of Daniel 3: Nebuchadnezzar the king made an image of gold, whose height was threescore cubits, and the breadth thereof six cubits: he set it up in the plain of Dura, in the province of Babylon. Saints a score (20), threescore cubits=60, breath there of (spirit) 6cubits.This symbolic meaning equals 66. Further according to Greek symbolism sigma is 6 and numeric value of 200. So entertaining this symbol three sigma's would be 600 and three score=60. Now altogether you get 660, well the number or last number you need is man or you.

2   Then Nebuchadnezzar the king sent to gather together the princes, the governors, and the captains, the judges, the treasurers, the counselors, the sheriffs, and all the rulers of the provinces, to come to the dedication of the image which Nebuchadnezzar the king had set up. Princes who are those daughters and sons inherited kingdoms, (President, Pope, Prince of
Countries), governors (Politicians), Captains (Attorney Generals), the Judges, treasurers (IRS)False Prophets, counselors (Lawyers and False prophets or Teachers), the sheriffs of the law, rulers of providence state officials. You

notice there are eight symbolic ranks of what, New Beginnings or also symbolic of New World Order Economically. Saints one last scenario there are currently 9 symbolic references the king makes is 9, there is only one King Yeshua, well Satan or Nebuchadnezzar name means Carnality 666, also Satan has only 9stones now since he was thrown out of heaven. The number 9 could also mean what spirit are you being operated under the 9 gifts of the fruits of the spirit or the opposite of them 9gifts of Carnality.

3 Then the princes, the governors, and captains, the judges, the treasurers, the counselors, the sheriffs, and all the rulers of the provinces, were gathered together unto the dedication of the image that Nebuchadnezzar the king had set up; and they stood before the image that Nebuchadnezzar had set up. [4] Then a herald cried aloud, To you it is commanded, O people, nations, and languages,

5 That at what time ye hear the sound of the cornet, flute, harp, sackbut, psaltery, dulcimer, and all kinds of music, ye fall down and worship the golden image that Nebuchadnezzar the king hath set up: You notice these instruments symbolically have six names, then states you ye fall down and worship. When you worship the Beast of Carnality you become the Mark of the beast 666.

6 And whoso falleth not down and worshippeth shall the same hour be cast into the midst of a burning fiery furnace. [7] Therefore at that time, when all the people heard the sound of the cornet, flute, harp, sackbut, psaltery, and all kinds of music, all the people, the nations, and the languages, fell down and worshiped the golden image that Nebuchadnezzar the king had set up. They were all burned alive whoever did not worship the beast.

According to the Islam rule and many Quotes you must submit to their conversion or be punished or die or it specifically states to fight them.

Look at the Deceit fullness in their own mindsets lost souls. They are controlled by a Spirit of Religion not of Yeshua Eyeh or The Holy Spirit.

Saints let's move on according to the scripture above there are three distinctive spirits above of symbolism's out of the 9. The Treasurer False teachers (Judas was a treasurer), Counselors False teachers, and also you have Nebuchadnezzar which could resemble spirit of Carnality just like Satan. Well the Unity of three which is the bad side resembled and now you have The Father
Eyeh asher Eyeh, Holy Spirit and Yeshua. You notice we are entering a new Tabernacle age or Eon age of creation. Immortality how you say well lets move on. Daniel 3:

12 There are certain Jews whom thou hast set over the affairs of the province of Babylon, Shadrach, Meshach, and Abednego; these men, O king, have not regarded thee: they serve not thy gods, nor worship the golden image which thou hast set up.

You notice there are three names symbolically, [17] If it be so, our God whom we serve is able to deliver us from the burning fiery furnace, and he will deliver us out of thine hand, O king.[18] But if not, be it known unto thee, O king, that we will not serve thy gods, nor worship the golden image which thou hast set up.

¹⁹   Then was Nebuchadnezzar full of fury, and the form of his visage was changed against Shadrach, Meshach, and Abednego: therefore he spake, and commanded that they should heat the furnace one seven times more than it was wont to be heated. You notice the furnace was Heated 7 more times, seven means Perfection. Eyeh rested on the 7th day of Creation.

²⁰   And he commanded the most mighty men that were in his army to bind Shadrach, Meshach, and Abednego, and to cast them into the burning fiery furnace. ²¹ Then these men were bound in their coats, their hosen, and their hats, and their other garments, and were cast into the midst of the burning fiery furnace.

²²   Therefore. because the king's commandment was urgent and the furnace exceeding hot, the flames of the fire slew those men that took up Shadrach, Meshach, and Abednego. Those who came up against the Presence of Eyeh who had the Shekinah Glory glory within them were destroyed immediately.

²³   And these three men, Shadrach, Meshach, and Abednego, fell down bound into the midst of the burning fiery furnace. ²⁴ Then Nebuchadnezzar the king was astonished, and rose up in haste, and spake, and said unto his counselors, Did not we cast three men bound into the midst of the fire? They answered and said unto the king, True, O king.

²⁵   He answered and said, Lo, I see four men loose, walking in the midst of the fire, and they have no hurt; and the form of the fourth is like the Son of God. The Son of Man which is the Ark the Rod and the Tabernacle

(Testimony) dwelt within inside man here on Earth. The 1,000 year reign immortality.

²⁶ Then Nebuchadnezzar came near to the mouth of the burning fiery furnace, and spake, and said, Shadrach, Meshach, and Abednego, ye servants of the most high God, come forth, and come hither. Then Shadrach, Meshach, and Abednego, came forth of the midst of the fire.

²⁷ And the princes, governors, and captains, and the king's counselors, being gathered together, saw these men, upon whose bodies the fire had no power, nor was an hair of their head singed, neither were their coats changed, nor the smell of fire had passed on them. The rulers of this earth or Kings of there kind of flame had no power over them.

²⁸ Then Nebuchadnezzar spake, and said, Blessed be the God of Shadrach, Meshach, and Abednego, who hath sent his angel, and delivered his servants that trusted in him, and have changed the king's word, and yielded their bodies, that they might not serve nor worship any god, except their own God.

²⁹ Therefore I make a decree, That every people, nation, and language, which speakany thing amiss against the God of Shadrach, Meshach, and Abednego, shall be cut in pieces, and their houses shall be made a dunghill: because there is no other God that can deliver after this sort.³⁰ Then the king promoted Shadrach, Meshach, and Abednego, in the province of Babylon. The opposite of the King Nebuchadnezzar or spirit is Yeshua's decree and

authorization of authority to rule and reign over the the rulers and officials of this earth.

Now you notice in my recent books I explained about the Tabernacle age Eon age, the Tabernacle the outer court 1500 cubits, inner court 10x20x10=2000 the church age which comes to 3,5oo years and coming to an end. The last entrance which man never full manifested the Tabernacle mystery is going through the veil the secrets mysteries the cherubim of the flaming sword, back to the Garden of Eden Immortality, the holy of holies 10x10x10 which equals 1,000 year reign. Well I am going to show you some symbolic meaning which I do not want you to digest but a similar ironic response. Notice Satan always loves to Pervert Yah's Significance.

CHAPTER 3

According to Buddhism According to some Buddhist traditions, the period of the Buddhist Law is divided into three stages: a first period of 500 years, of the turning the Wheel of the Law; a second period of 1,000 years, of the deterioration of the Law, and a third period of 3,000 years (called Mappo in Japan) during which no one practices the Law. After this, Buddhism having disappeared, a new Buddha will appear who will again turn the Wheel of the Law.

This future Buddha is still in the (Tusita heaven), in the state of a Bodhisattva. Gautama Buddha himself will enthrone him as his successor. The name means 'benevolence' or 'friendship'. He is now living his last existence as a Bodhisattva. In anticipation of his imminent arrival, he is sometimes considered as a Buddha and given the title of Tathagata.The Celestial body of Heaven will enthrone himself with the earthly human.

According to the word Buddha Maitreya The Purpose of Christ is to increase the Light of the Soul on the Earth. My Yoga is to manifest the energy of Heaven into the Earth, you notice earth is us. According to their rituals, this picture below is nothing but ritual or grade of spectrum according to their pagan rituals but showing you as a comparison how Satan loves to Pervert Yah's Significances.

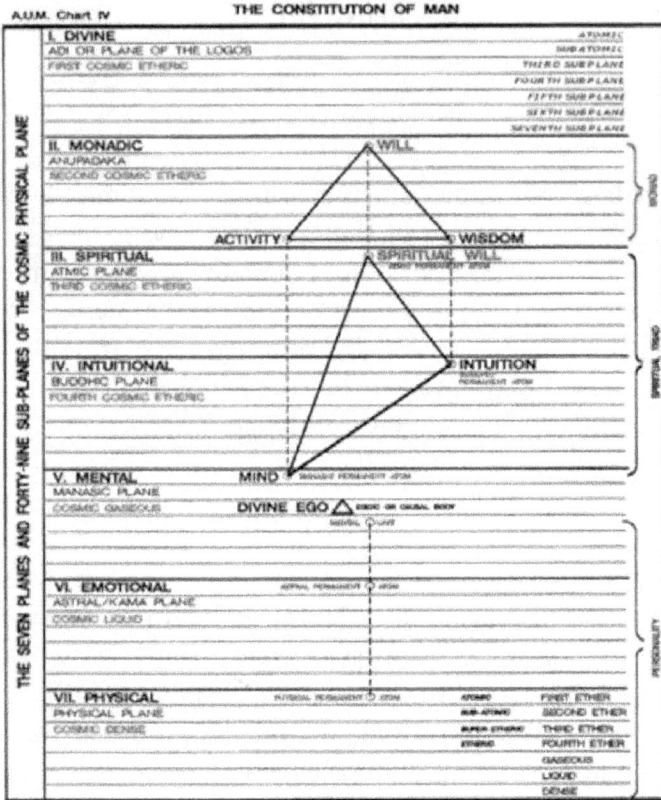

A.U.M. Chart IV — THE CONSTITUTION OF MAN

You notice this graph has seven planes which also means perfection. Eyeh rested on the Seventh Day. This graph is explaining the basic atomic level plane. The atomic level of an atom or subatomic levels unite as one becoming the creative light. The physical form has a cosmic unity to become Gaseous like a Cloud, Yah's shekinah glory Liquid form Yeshua walked on water, then it states Dense which is matter submitting under your feet or Authority walking in Complete Dominion. Now everything I shown as Buddha and Maitreya or the the Diagram graph I am not digesting at all but just using it as a scenario of ironic comparison.

Now Continuing of this Revelations revealed how the Muslims got their God From pagan rituals. A gilded metal plate showing the Greek goddess Cybele, ca. 200 BC, from one of the Greek colonies founded in Afghanistan in the aftermath of Alexander's conquests. In the bible Genesis 1: And God said, Let there be lights in the firmament of the heaven to divide the day from the night; and let them be for signs, and for seasons, and for days, and years. Season in Hebrews means appointed times Moedim fixed festival or meeting place. You can also see that Satan always loves to pervert Eyeh Asher Eyeh's teachings and symbols. You notice shes riding on a lion. Just like Yeshua returns the Lion of the tribe of Judah. You also notice the symbol of the Statue of Liberty same Deity.

This Picture is also located in the Roman Catholic Church.

According to the Bible Noah's Great Grandson was Nimrod who died and called the Sun God he was a great Hunter. He was Deified name was called Baal his wife Sumeramis, Baal wasn't ready for her, Sent her back into Earth as Egg, Pagans believe that Earth was birthed out of an Egg, So when they sent her forth they turned a Bird into a Rabbit that lays eggs. Every Year on the First Sunday sunrise of the Spring Equinox, the Priest of Ishtar would impregnate virgin women and also sacrifice 3month old baby's and dip the eggs into the blood. That is where you get Easter. Astharoth is Easter, the Great Babylon, is the Antichrist and the Multitudes.

The King and Queen of Heaven Egypt Osiris and Isis, Phoenica-Baal and Ashteroth,Greece-Adonis and Aphrodite,Assyria-Asher and Ishtar, Persia-Mithra and Anahita,Rome-Apollo and Diana/Cybele. They call Mary the Queen of Heaven. In the Catholic church they have Mary and the son of God which is not Mary and Jesus. It's the Trinity of Satanic Symbol, below is the Pic.

The "Entire" Earth is Lying in the Power of Ancient Babylon and the spell cast by Nimrod and his mother.

SEMIRAMIS got pregnant and claimed it to be a gift from the gods, the reincarnation of Nimrod, when, in fact, it was the result of a betrayal, since her husband and son was already dead. And TAMMUZ was born on Dec. 25, the sun-god of the Egyptians, Babylonians, Greeks, Persians, Romans, and today, from the SS (secret societies). He died during a hunting trip, probably by a wild animal, and his body was found lying on a rotten tree trunk. His mother said that a pine tree sprout from the rotten trunk and every year, on the 25th of December, it was common for people to take a pine tree home and decorate it with gold and silver, as a symbol of the rebirth of Tammuz.

The priestesses fasted and wept for 40 days and 40 nights over the death of TAMMUZ at the foot of the pine tree, and once finished, they thanked each other by exchanging gifts, which were deposited at the foot of the pine tree. Every year, on the 25th of December, Christmas was celebrated (the birth of Tammuz).

The priestesses fasted and wept for 40 days and 40 nights over the death of TAMMUZ at the foot of the pine tree, and once finished, they thanked each other by exchanging gifts, which were deposited at the foot of the pine tree. Every year, on the 25th of December, Christmas was celebrated (the birth of Tammuz).

When the PERSIANS dominated this region, they took all of their idols back to PERSIA, including the gods TAMMUZ, NIMROD and SEMIRAMIS, and simply changed their names. The GREEKS soon gained power and they did the same thing, by changing their names. They became ZEUS, APHRODITE AND EROS.

Then the Egyptians gained power and changed their names as well. They became OSIRIS, ISIS
AND HORUS.

But during the times of JESUS CHRIST, ROME was in power and they also changed their names. They became known as VENUS AND CUPID, because the father figure was dropped. During the fourth century after Christ, to please the Christians, who were in large numbers in ROME, Emperor CONSTANTINE decided to honor Christianity, making it the official religion of ROME. To please them even more, he took the strongest names within Christianity and began to give the idols CHRISTIAN NAMES.

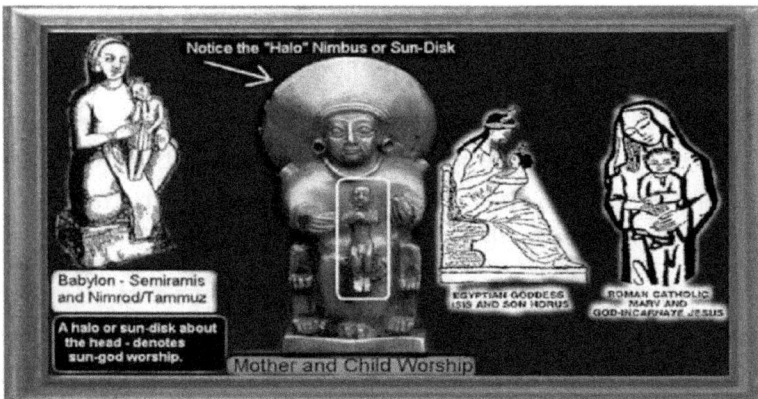

Saints Lets consider this in the bible verse about Christmas in Detail. Jeremiah 10: Hear ye the word which the LORD speaketh unto you, O house of Israel:[2] Thus saith the LORD, Learn not the way of the heathen, and be not dismayed at the signs of heaven; for the heathen are dismayed at them.[3] For the customs of the people are vain: for one cutteth a tree out of the forest, the work of the hands of the workman, with the axe.[4] They deck it with silver and with gold; they fasten it with nails and with hammers, that it move not.[5] They are upright as the palm tree, but speak not: they must needs be borne, because they cannot go. Be not afraid of them; for they cannot do evil, neither also is it in them to do good.[6] Forasmuch as there is none like unto thee, O LORD; thou art great, and thy name is great in might.

You notice the Vatican has Tammuz Deity, the serpent Satan, the Moon Goddess Hindu God Shiva, Inside the Dome of the Rock pagan Symbols. In Roman times, she was called Diana and became associated with the moon, virginity and fertility, as well as animas, and became known as the mother of all Gods, the Queen of Heaven. She was the daughter of Zeus and her brother was Apollos. She then became a symbol or name called Cybele in a few picture above, her riding in here chariot pulled by lions and represented by a crescent moon and star, which is the black meteorite that "fell from heaven". On page 13 of this book.

Acts 19: [22] So he sent into Macedonia two of them that ministered unto him, Timotheus and Erastus; but he himself stayed in Asia for a season.[23] And the same time there arose no small stir about that way.[24] For a certain man named Demetrius, a silversmith, which made silver shrines for Diana, brought no small gain unto the craftsmen;[25] Whom he called together with the workmen of like occupation, and said, Sirs, ye know that by this craft we have our wealth.

26 Moreover ye see and hear, that not alone at Ephesus, but almost throughout all Asia, this Paul hath persuaded and turned away much people, saying that they be no gods, which are made with hands:[27] So that not only this our craft is in danger to be set at nought; but also that the temple of the great goddess Diana should be despised, and her magnificence should be destroyed, whom all Asia and the world worshippeth. So Buddhism came from Asia Deity paganism adopted by Muslims.

Paul is speaking of silver gold and wood and messing with the Stock Market in the Book of Acts.

[35] And when the town clerkk had appeesed the people, he said, Ye men of Ephesus, what man is there that knoweth not how that the city of the Ephesians is a worshipper of the great goddess Diana, and of the image which fell down from Jupiter? Here is another illustration of the Bible

[35] And when the town clerk had quieted the crowd, he said, "Men of Ephesus, who is there who does not know that the city of the Ephesians is temple keeper of the great Artemis, and of the sacred stone that fell from the sky?

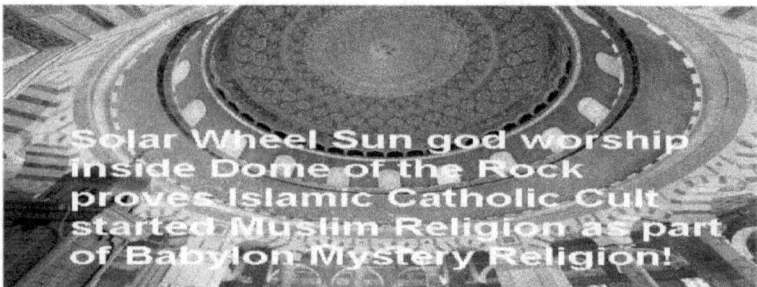

Solar Wheel Sun god worship inside Dome of the Rock proves Islamic Catholic Cult started Muslim Religion as part of Babylon Mystery Religion!

Aphrodite at Paphos, Cybele at Pessinus and later Rome, Astarte at Byblos and the famous Artemis/Diana of Ephesus all were known for a black stone being associated with their worship.

In 204 Ad the black stone was moved to Rome where it stayed until it was lost in the 5th century. Muhammad Took Mecca 632 AD. The Kah ba Stone, was dedicated to Hubal, a Nabatean deity, and idols which either represented the days of the year, or were effigies of the Arabian pantheon. According to Ibn Ishaq, an early biographer of Muhammad, the Ka'aba was itself addressed as a female Deity, three generations before the advent of Islam. – Islam: A short History, Karen Armstrong-Wikipedia.

Om Namah Shivaya Sanskrit Symbol. When you break down these symbols the numeric value becomes 786, remember everything speaks of Characters and functions. The Hindu Sacred number is 786 and Islam where they come from the Sacred number is 786. If you take the first sentence and add up the letters in Arabic it comes out to 786, Muhammad adopted the Hindu religion

Only 786

KHAUD KE SAATH EK RUHANI RISHTA

Saints Hello what became their God!

The Origin Of Islamic Symbol : 786

786 is known to be the symbolic representation of the word Allah but no Islamic scholar so far has been able to explain why and how this 786 came to be in Islam....

Now let me show you something Very Interesting Saints love you all. Until this day no Scholar from there nation Cannot figure where and why does this numeric value come from at all. I am going to show you this definition and understanding of Revelation in Complete Detail some more by the Grace of Yeshua. Do you see all the Points Coming together all in one Piece. That is why Yah does not like us to worship or practice Pagan Holidays at all.

Saintsrophecy that was given by (Yawn Al-Ghadab, Safar Alhwaly), the true Messiah who is the islamic Mahdi,will defeat Europe, will lead this army of Seljuks, He will Preside over the world from Jerusalem because Mecca would have been Destroyed. Now consider this factor their own prophecy gives precise interpretation that mecca will be destroyed. Isaiah 34:6 The sword of the Lord is filled with blood [of sacrifices], it is gorged *and* greased with fatness—with the blood of lambs and goats, with the fat of the kidneys of rams. For the Lord has a sacrifice in Bozrah [capital of Edom] and a great slaughter in the land of Edom.7 And the wild oxen shall fall with them, and the [young] bullocks with the [old and mighty] bulls; and their land shall be drunk *and* soaked with blood, and their dust made rich with fatness.8 For the Lord has a day of vengeance, a year of recompense, for the cause of Zion.9 And the streams [of Edom] will be turned into pitch and its dust into brimstone, and its land will become burning pitch.

The only thing that can burn is Petroleum, if you dump it into streams it is oil. Revelation 18:8And the kings of the earth(other Countries who benefited off of her), who have committed fornication and lived deliciously with her, shall bewail her, and lament for her, when they shall see the smoke of her burning,10 Standing afar off for the fear of her torment, saying, Alas, alas, that great city Babylon, that mighty city! for in one hour is thy judgment come,11And the merchants of the earth weep and mourn for her, since no one buys their cargo anymore,12The merchandise of gold, and silver, and precious stones, and of pearls, and fine linen, and purple, and silk, and scarlet, and all thine wood, and all manner vessels of ivory, and all manner vessels of most precious wood, and of brass, and iron, and marble. Only oil burns, it creates great smoke, great Babylon that might city, the city of Oil.

The 9 cities in the desert that carry the oil which were Muhammad planted his Kingdom in Mecca, there also next to the sea shore. No more cargo-merchandise carried by ships.13And cinnamon, and odors, and ointments, and frankincense, and wine, and oil, and fine flour, and wheat, and beasts, and sheep, and horses, and chariots, and slaves, and souls of men,14 And the fruits that thy soul lusted after are departed from thee, and all things which were dainty and goodly are departed from thee, and thou shalt find them no more at all,15The merchants of these things, who were made rich by her, shall stand afar off for the fear of her torment, weeping and wailing,16 And saying, Alas, alas, that great city, that was clothed in fine linen, and purple, and scarlet, and decked with gold, and precious stones, and pearls!

You notice two more verses 17In one hour such great wealth has been brought to ruin!' "Every sea captain, and all who travel by ship, the sailors, and all who earn their living from the sea, will stand far off,18They will cry out as they watch the smoke ascend, and they will say, "Where is there another city as great as this?"19 They will throw dust on their heads, and with weeping and mourning cry out: "'Woe! Woe to you, great city, where all who had ships on the sea became rich through her wealth! In one hour she has been brought to ruin!'

You notice they threw dust on their Head, some say America is the Great Babylon, no the Arab countries who have desert waste lands, only would throw dust on their heads not eastern or western America. It is their territory that is so significance to the great wealth. The Prophet (peace be upon him) said: The flourishing state of Jerusalem will be when Yathrib (Medina) is in ruins, the ruined state of Yathrib will be when the great war come..(Sunan of Abu Dawud Book 37, Number 4281: Narrated Muwadh ibn jabal.Mecca and Medina will be destroyed, they are both in Saudi Arabia.

Lets give you some Scripture on this Isaiah 13:19 And Babylon, the glory of kingdoms, the beauty of the Chaldean s' pride, shall be like Sodom and Gomorrah when God overthrew them.20 [Babylon] shall never be inhabited or dwelt in from generation to generation; neither shall the Arab pitch his tent there, nor shall the shepherds make their sheepfolds there. It specifically stated Arab nation.

Jeremiah 47:7 Concerning *and* against Edom: Thus says the Lord of hosts: Is there no longer wisdom in Teman [a district in Edom]? Has counsel vanished from the intelligent *and* prudent? Is their wisdom all poured out *and* used up?8 Flee, turn back, dwell deep [in the deserts to escape the Chaldeans], O inhabitants of Dedan [neighbor of Edom]! For I will bring the calamity *and* destruction of Esau upon him [Edom] when I inspect *and* punish him.

19 Behold, one will come up like a lion from the [o]thickets of the Jordan against [p]a perennially watered

pasture; for in an instant I will make him run away from it, and whoever is chosen I shall appoint over it. For who is like Me, and who will summon Me *into court*? And who then is the shepherd who can stand against Me?"

20 Therefore hear the plan of the LORD which He has planned against Edom, and His purposes which He has purposed against the inhabitants of Teman: surely they will drag them off, *even* the little ones of the flock; surely He will make their [q]pasture desolate because of them. 21 The earth has quaked at the noise of their downfall. There is an outcry! The noise of it has been heard at the [r]Red Sea. 22 Behold, [s]He will mount up and swoop like an eagle and spread out His wings [t]against Bozrah; and the hearts of the mighty men of Edom in that day will be like the heart of a woman in labor. Arabian Peninsula Destroyed.

Isaiah 21:21 The burden of the Desert of the Sea: As whirlwinds in the South pass through, so it cometh from the desert, from a terrible land. 9 And behold, here cometh a chariot of men with a couple of horsemen!" And he answered and said, "Babylon is fallen, is fallen! And all the graven images of her gods He hath broken unto the ground!" 13 The burden upon Arabia: In the forest in Arabia shall ye lodge, O ye traveling companies of Dedanites. Wow Saints the Book of Revelation is the Great Mystery Babylon judgment against the oiled lands.

In Saudi Arabia you have Duba, Tasuk, Medina, Yanbu, Mecca, Taif, Abha, Jizan and Jedua. You also notice Satan has only 9stones instead of 12stones. Lets move on Revelation 12:3 And there appeared another wonder in heaven: behold, a great red dragon, having seven heads and ten horns, and seven crowns upon his heads. The

Prince of this world the Great Babylon, with the Satan and ruling governments of this world against the Jews and the Church Body of Christ. Isaiah 27:In that day, the LORD will punish with his sword-- his fierce, great and powerful sword-- Leviathan the gliding serpent, Leviathan the coiling serpent; he will slay the monster of the sea. The Serpent is Satan an a resemblance of a Spirit.

Here is another interpretation of Revelation 12:6 And the woman fled into the wilderness, where she hath a place prepared by God, that they should feed her there a thousand two hundred and threescore days. This number comes out to 1,260 or 1,290. This mystery has been recorded in my other books, there are four scenarios of revelations in this passage. The first one up above I gave you the symbol pics page 18,19,now I am going to refer them in the 666 Mark of the Beast form and how it relates to Scripture also. The Hindu God of Shiva Buddhism symbol, Allah symbol.

The first one states 1,290 days, if you add 1+2=9 equals 12 and the zero in back 120, it took Noah 120 years for Noah to build and ark, meaning a new day of creation and a transitional shift, an end at hand. The second is 1,260 why, two symbolic meanings well a score is (20), also threescore means according to Hebrew Calendar they have 30 day months. Further the continuing of the second it says a thousand which can be one 6,then it states two hundred, now according to sigma 6 is value is 200x3 gives you 600, and then it states threescore (20) that comes out to 60 which then equals 666. Well recapture page 18,19 to understand the resemblance. Lets move on the third you can count 1+2+6=9 with zero in back 90. Watch carefully well you notice also in the book of Daniel it states 1,290 days also states the abomination of desolation comes to an end. Well you ad 1+2=3 divided by 90 gives you 30 or 30 minutes which is an Half hour correct. Revelation 8:1 And when he had opened the seventh seal, there was silence in heaven about the space of half an hour.

We are coming into a Divine shift in History Saints. Now watch this the Hindu God and practices The vedangas known as the limbs of the Vedas are six in number (sikhsa, kalpa, vyakarna, nirukta, chandasa and chitihi. The tantras are aslo six. In the brahmanas a Brahman is prescribed six fold duties: teaching, studying, performing sacrifice, offering sacrifice and charity. A king in ancient india was allowed to receive one sixth of produce from the farmers as his share. Ancient magicians performed six acts of magic: creating peace, deluding, immobilizing, creating enmity, ruining an enemy and causing death. There are six Hindu schools of Philosophy: Samkhya, yoga, nyaya, vaisheshika, purva and uttara mimansa and vedanta. The six sided hexagon is a symbol of Durga and used in the tantric symbols. Katyani, an aspect of Durga is Kwon as shashti. Married couple perform shastifpurthi, almost another marriage function, when the husband attains 60 years of age while the wife is till alive.

You notice seducing spirits always try to replicate what Yah has done in purity and they try to twist it. The Great Babylon, explains that Babel means confusion. Leviticus 26:1 Ye shall make you no idols nor graven image, neither rear you up a standing image, neither shall ye set up *any* image of stone in your land, to bow down unto it: for I *am* the LORD your God. Muslims worship false God, they even have the first five book of Moses in their Qauran and should recap what the book of Leviticus says.

Saints the heavenly father has cracked opened the six seal

in the book of Revelation, there was a major earthquake in Nepal over 5,000 to 9,000 possibly dead. In Nepal, people worship crows and cows, dogs and snakes, vehicles and tools. They even worship Pagan Gods Hindu and many others.

Most of them worship pagan witchcraft idols and they received a consequence. The Religious false doctrine is being revitalized and corrected through understanding. In my Walk and Yielding to Revelation there has been many sermons or teachings that were taught out of humanism. Such as Back lash and Retaliation, No such Psychological Counterfeit of this, Psalms 28 verse [7] The Lord is my Strength and my [impenetrable] Shield; my heart trusts in, relies on, *and* confidently leans on Him, and I am helped; therefore my heart greatly rejoices, and with my song will I praise Him.

Psalms 29

[11] The Lord will give [unyielding and impenetrable] strength to His people; the Lord will bless His people with peace. The father gives Impenetrable and Untraceable protection........

1st Corinthians 13:12

[12] For now we are looking in a mirror that gives only a dim (blurred) reflection [of reality as [e]in a riddle or enigma], but then [when perfection comes] we shall see in reality *and* face to face! Now I know in part (imperfectly), but then I shall know *and* understand [f]fully *and* clearly, even in the same manner as I have been [g]fully *and* clearly

known *and* understood [[h]by God]. We shall come to understanding just as the same manner as we have been fully and clearly known and understood by God.

Our Eyes Shall see Like our Father sees meaning our Understanding, Wisdom & Knowledge.

Matthew 5

[48] You, therefore, must be perfect [growing into complete [ak]maturity of godliness in mind and character, [al]having reached the proper height of virtue and integrity], as your heavenly Father is perfect.

Trials and Tribulations come to an end Completely and you enter into Divine Rest!

Isaiah 51

[16] And I have put My words in your mouth and have covered you with the shadow of My hand, that I may fix the [new] heavens as a tabernacle and lay the foundations of a [new] earth and say to Zion, You are My people. New Heavens as a Tabernacle (Immortality), new Earth a Transitional State of Enlightenment And Promise land Of A New Earth Understood by Revelation.

[17] Arouse yourself, awake! Stand up, O Jerusalem, you who have drunk at the hand of the Lord the cup of His wrath, you who have drunk the cup of staggering *and* intoxication to the dregs. [18] There is none to guide her among all the sons she has borne; neither is there anyone to take her by the hand among all the sons whom she has brought up.

¹⁹   Two kinds of calamities have befallen you—but who feels sorry for *and* commiserates you?— they are desolation and destruction [on the land and city], and famine and sword [on the inhabitants]—how shall I comfort you *or* by whom?

²⁰   Your sons have fainted; they lie [like corpses] at the head of all the streets, like an antelope in a net; they are full [from drinking] of the wrath of the Lord, the rebuke of your God.

²¹   Therefore, now hear this, you who are afflicted, and [who are] drunk, but not with wine [but thrown down by the wrath of God].

²²   Thus says your Lord, the Lord, and your God, Who pleads the cause of His people: Behold, I have taken from your hand the cup of staggering *and* intoxication; the cup of My wrath you shall drink no more.

²³   And I will put it into the hands of your tormentors *and* oppressors, those who said to you, Bow down, that we may ride *or* tread over you; and you have made your back like the ground and like the street for them to pass over.

Jeremiah 33

⁷   Behold, [in the future restored Jerusalem] I will lay upon it health and healing, and I will cure them and will reveal to them the abundance of peace (prosperity, security, stability) and truth. ⁷ And I will cause the captivity of Judah and the captivity of Israel to be reversed and will rebuild them as they were at first.

[8] And I will cleanse them from all the guilt *and* iniquity by which they have sinned against Me, and I will forgive all their guilt *and* iniquities by which they have sinned and rebelled against Me.

[9] And [Jerusalem] shall be to Me a name of joy, a praise and a glory before all the nations of the earth that hear of all the good I do for it, and they shall fear and tremble because of all the good and all the peace, prosperity, security, *and* stability I provide for it.

The things that the world is trying to accomplish will not succeed, those whose oppose him Daddy Yahweh the Father the Son and the Holy spirit within us will be Burned saved by fire or Torched by his Wrath. The world system will not be able to Stand in the Presence of His Children his Remnant!

Daniel 7

[10] A stream of fire came forth from before Him; a thousand thousands ministered to Him and ten thousand times ten thousand rose up *and* stood before Him; the Judge was seated [the court was in session] and the books were opened. New order, New Revelation, New understanding, A Ruler ship of His Kingdom ruling Nations Having full Complete Dominion over the Earth and the Galaxies. Myriads of Myriads of Angels, Behold Yeshua comes with Ten thousand of His Saints. The Remnant Saints. When A Judge sits and Enthrones Himself within you the World and Galaxies are Governed The Fathers Way Line upon Line Precept upon Precept!

CHAPTER 4

OK saints, I am not Judging anyone at all. but my other Books spoke of Keen discernment and Discerning of Spirits, The Highly intellectual Psychological Warfare on Most Gospel Channels, you have no clue how to discern what spirit is operating cause you're not there yet not even close. Just being real, I'm not gonna start naming the people and titles cause you would think possibly in a carnal way about what im trying to expose. The next page or next paragraph your going to see or experience are just a sign of Discerning of Spirits, what goes on that most of you have no clue of. All you see is anointing or great name or title and you run to it, or possibly you already have been bewitched with false doctrine and its excepted beyond your will cause your either bound by it already or in self-denial or you have excepted your Prophets or leaders of Personal gain or your just desperate and naive.

The Darkest Side of Cindy Trimm: Strong Satanic Prayer you tube video. Watch the hand signs. Man trons: Evil counterparts of the Astralborgs. Created by Les Fortunes as a child to rival Art Fortunes' Astralborgs in their only collaboration, the Lost Comic. Time 4:41-43 The spirit of Ast Astral. Then I Hear the spirit say Man trons or Matrons are being extended. The spirit did not say Mantles. The time 5:43 matrons are being extended. You notice she called forth spirits from the grave Matrons, and the spirit of Ast and other spirits. God Open Cindy Trimms eyes and bless her.

You notice the spirit said Trailblazers in the spirit realm, Blazers are considered Badges of Territorial Demons from different sectors of the Fallen angel Kingdoms. You notice the Spirit said I call it from the grave, meaning if you open up your heart to me and receive my spirit of witchcraft I will give you Prosperity and business and Finances and your sons and daughters from the prisons and crack houses will worship me also and have these treasures.

The Bible speaks of Demon Spirits just as in the Book of Daniel, The Father decreed it the Correct One True God Yah, Eyeh asher Eyeh. Daniel 4:28 All this happened to King Nebuchadnezzar. 29 Twelve months later, as the king was walking on the roof of the royal palace of Babylon, 30 he said, "Is not this the great Babylon I have built as the royal residence, by my mighty power and for the glory of my majesty?"

31 Even as the words were on his lips, a voice came from heaven, "This is what is decreed for you, King Nebuchadnezzar: Your royal authority has been taken from you. 32 You will be driven away from people and will

live with the wild animals; you will eat grass like the ox. Seven times will pass by for you until you acknowledge that the Most High is sovereign over all kingdoms on earth and gives them to anyone he wishes."

33 Immediately what had been said about Nebuchadnezzar was fulfilled. He was driven away from people and ate grass like the ox. His body was drenched with the dew of heaven until his hair grew like the feathers of an eagle and his nails like the claws of a bird. There are videos already Mocking The Father doing the Harlem shake and moving in the gifts of the spirit by mocking. Also another video show churches preaching Yeshua was naked on the cross and left the tomb Naked and the Minister is naked preaching and other members all naked reading the word of God. These malicious spirits are all here. Already False Prophet from Africa made the people eat grass all of them.

The symbolism of eating grass like a wild beast, having Carnal functions as a wild animal and soulish power. The bible speaks about having Character, and many times being clothed. Carnality, ignorance, False doctrine and Angel of light spirits being manifested right in front of our very eyes, but do not have the Discernment to discern what spirit is operating or asking about the motive and intentions of the Heart.

Saints according to Isaiah 55:1"Come, all you who are thirsty, come to the waters;and you who have no money, come, buy and eat!Come, buy wine and milk without money and without cost.2 Why spend money on what is not bread,and your labor on what does not satisfy?Listen, listen to me, and eat what is good, and you will delight in the richest of fare. Saints Buy in Hebrew means to Redeem and receive his goodness and eat. Saints in congregations are spending money on what is not true pure doctrine (Bread revelation, meat, mana). Saints Labor (Tithe comes from labor which does not satisfy the father). The father want you to know him as the self who he is, so you need to know yourself and see yourself as he sees you, we need continuance of self revelation and come to the end of ourselves completely.

Saints let me give you some more understanding of Fresh Revelation, Joel 2:23 Be glad then, you children of Zion, and rejoice in the LORD your God: for he has given you the former rain faithfully, and he will cause to come down for you the rain, the former rain, and the latter rain in the first month.

New living translation be glad, people of Zion, rejoice in the LORD your God, for he has given you the autumn rains because he is faithful. He sends you abundant showers, both autumn and spring rains, as before. What happens in autumn and spring, there is set time and shift and setback, when there is a setback there is also a shooting forth of time of speed magnified into the now form. You notice he said the former and the latter rain in the first month. There is a consummation of seasons that come together as one. Faith is the substance of things hoped for, for love worketh faith, Faith is Eternal, Infinite it always is a knowing. Time is past, present and future so time has not caught up with faith the belief and knowing of the time, spiritual timing.

Matthew 24: Jesus left the temple and was walking away when his disciples came up to him to call his attention to its buildings. 2 "Do you see all these things?" he asked. "Truly I tell you, not one stone here will be left on another; everyone will be thrown down."

3 As Jesus was sitting on the Mount of Olives, the disciples came to him privately. "Tell us," they said, "when will this happen, and what will be the sign of your coming and of the end of the age?"

When has to do with time and the Timing of the Holy spirit, three dimensions in God, that is given clarity of signs, wonders and miracles. Outer court, Inner court, Holy of Holies, signs are to the world, Moses went to Pharaoh he went with signs and wonders but not miracles. Signs are an outer court manifestation that means everyone can see what is visible and plain. The church is at a deficit of true Prophecy, we have a lot of speculation, gibbered intelligence as we call prognosis, and church relies on prognosis. They do not want to hear the Prophet or Apostle at all they are removed. The interpretation of mysteries of God and the Council of God is hidden from the Church once they are removed. The job of the Apostle and Prophet is to Interpret Revelation of mysteries and his Council in Glory.

The Prophet will interpret the Universe and Times; we are at a Deficit of Revelation and Prophecy. Meaning the church runs from anything that is Prophetic and Great Heavy Hailstones and Talents. My People are destroyed for lack of Knowledge, if true Interpretation function correctly how could there be misunderstanding and division and no unity. Your victory is tied to your Knowing, Your defeat is tied to your ignorance even self-denial and rebellion to see and perceive self. Even the weather Patents are not in

Order, everything that can be shaken will be shaken, even the weather, nothing is not going to be in its place of origin. It means we are entering a season that is going against reason and explanation.

Haggai 2:6 for thus says the LORD of hosts; yet once, it is a little while, and I will shake the heavens, and the earth, and the sea, and the dry land. Hebrew 12:26 whose voice then shook the earth: but now he has promised, saying, yet once more I shake not the earth only, but also heaven. He has identified the Year of Promise and Promises of his True Nature; His Sovereignty has stepped forth into the Natural here on Earth. Sovereignty-the status, dominion, power, or authority of a sovereign; royal rank or position; royalty. The Interpretation of Weather shifts cannot be found in weather man, it cannot be found in the lips of Scientists. That means everything that is logic and common sense will be burned out by fire of his transforming revelation of understanding. The bible in the Realm of Prophecy is written to three people, the Jew, than the church then the world. None of their timings are the same; there are two people on the earth. The mind of God, two creations on the earth, there is two Adams walked the earth. If you're not born again and not saved you are in the first atom. Most of prophecy that we read would to apply to you, because Adam is still being judged. The second atom birthed a new creation he birthed a new man, he birthed a new breed.

When God made Adam and placed him in the Garden, the first Adam as powerful as he was, he was not made to know the Future. If he was made to know the future he would have seen the fall. What was Adam made to know, why he lived in the Glory of God and His Power he was made to live in the Now. So when the Second Adam came, to restore not the future but the Now. Anytime you're looking for something to happen it has happened and it is already done and is it already written. That means you're still in the first Adam. The Feasts represents the cycle of Gods Economy, that's why all the Feasts that we are told to observe, that's why they are all around Harvest. There are certain Prophecies, assigned to certain Feasts. This lets you know exactly, where we are in the Time of God, in the Plan and Purpose of God. We don't have the amount of time everyone is talking about. There is a Discrepancy in the Church you are either going to be in Prophecy or in the Feasts. When Egypt was being judged Israel kept the Feasts. If the church does not Keep the Feasts, there is stuff that's going to happen to you that is not supposed to happen to you cause you don't know there purpose and timings.

I don't understand how Christians are going through the same thing world is going through. Every miracle that Yeshua did was to enforce original intent. Do you know why He multiplied bread and fish? cause lack was not original intent. Do you know why he healed the sick, because Sickness, the lame, blind, cancer, deaf and dumbness was not his original intent? If it's not original intent than its called Disorder. The first five books he taught Parables in Revelation, He told Peter one time get thee behind me Satan, James and John at one point in the bible, after they could not cast out a certain spirit, they argued who was the greatest and also wanted to call fire from heaven and kill some people.

Luke 9: Then Jesus called together the Twelve [apostles] and gave them power and authority over all demons, and to cure diseases, 2 And He sent them out to announce *and* preach the kingdom of God and to bring healing. Announce means to Declare, Preach in Hebrew means Qara; bewray self that are bidden. Bewray means divulge, betray- to deliver or expose to an enemy by treachery or disloyalty. Expose your hidden self, that Yeshua may be glorified Christ the Hope of Glory within you to come out of his character and understanding. Yeshua taught 70 parables in the first Five books, it was all revelation then what happened after the first five Gospels. He gave the authority, dominion and Power. What happened at Pentecost hello Power fell Shekinah Glory, what fell Understanding of Revelation truth not just truth.

Verse 3 and He said to them, Do not take anything for your journey—neither walking stick, nor [a]wallet [for a collection bag], nor food of any kind, nor money, and do not have two undergarments (tunics). Hello how are they supposed to collect the Tithe with no wallet or collection bag?

Verse 12 Now the day began to decline, and the Twelve came and said to Him, Dismiss the crowds *and* send them away, so that they may go to the neighboring hamlets *and* villages and the surrounding country and find lodging and get a [b]supply of provisions, for we are here in an uninhabited (barren, solitary) place. 13 But He said to them, you [yourselves] give them [food] to eat. They said, We have no more than five loaves and two fish—unless we are to go and buy food for all this crowd, Now you're asking how come the Apostles Did not understand what was stated. Yeshua's understanding had no reason, logic or common sense in him at all. Provision means original intent of God, it also means, A particular requirement in a law, rule, agreement, or document. He gave Adam dominion over the Earthly realm, Galatians

4:8 formerly, when you did not know God, and you were slaves to those who by nature are not gods. 9 But now that you know God—or rather are known by God—how is it that you are turning back to those weak and miserable forces[d]? Do you wish to be enslaved by them all over again? 10 You are observing special days and months and seasons and years! 11 I fear for you, that somehow I have wasted my efforts on you. One day Sunday Zeus Monday is moon day, Tuesday is Tius day in Latin which is mars, Wednesday widens day mercury, Thursday which is thors day of Jupiter, Friday is Venus or Aphrodite, and Saturday is Saturn or Chronos pagan god. Birthdays the God of Time that is an idol, it is its own entity, old age, months the calendar year cycle God Time, Zeus the Sun God. The Moon which is season which also has to due with time Night time, which is an idol, hello Muslims bow down to appointed full moons. Hello Saints it says seasons summer, winter, spring, fall events created by mankind, Easter, Halloween, Christmas, 4th of July, **Maia** (Greek) The Goddess of Spring represented the forces of growth and the return of the warm rays of the sun.

Oh really Saints watch this in the book of Joshua 10:12 Then spake Joshua to the LORD in the day when the LORD delivered up the Amorites before the children of Israel, and he said in the sight of Israel, Sun, stand thou still upon Gibeon; and thou, Moon, in the valley of Ajalon.He had authority and dominion over the sun god and moon god cycle. The year god is God of Nature Earth, wind, water and Fire. Now let's go back to Luke 9:28 now about eight days after these teachings, Jesus took with Him Peter and John and James and went up on the mountain to pray.

You notice verse 26 because whoever is ashamed of me and of my teachings, of him will the Son of Man be ashamed when He comes in the [[l]threefold] glory (the splendor and majesty) of Himself and of the Father and of the holy angels. You notice it says ashamed of my Teachings of his Revelations. I will be ashamed of him.

38 And behold, a man from the crowd shouted out, Master, I implore You to look at my son, for he is my only child; 39 And behold, a spirit seizes him and suddenly he cries out; it convulses him so that he foams at the mouth; and he is sorely shattered, and it will scarcely leave him.40 And I implored Your disciples to drive it out, but they could not.

41 Jesus answered, O [faithless ones] unbelieving *and* without trust in God, a perverse ([o]wayward, [p]crooked and [q]warped) generation! Until when *and* how long am I to be with you and bear with you? Bring your son here [to me]. Perverse means unclean double minded, hopelessness, doubt, fear unbelieving, wayward -following one's own capricious, wanton, or depraved inclinations, following no clear principle or law-opposite to what is desired or expected. Not my will O Lord But thy will be done!. Synonym for crooked is twisted Doctrine or teaching, warped also means twisted or distortion of the truth.

52 And He sent messengers before Him; and they reached and entered a Samaritan village to make [things] ready for Him; 53 But [the people] would not welcome *or* receive *or* accept Him, because His face was [set as if He was] going to Jerusalem.

54 And when His disciples James and John observed this, they said, Lord, do You wish us to command fire to come down from heaven and consume them, [s]*even as Elijah did*?55 But He turned and rebuked *and* severely censured them. [t]*He said, you do not know of what sort of spirit you are, you notice they could not cast out a certain spirit because they had the same unclean spirit. 58 And Jesus told him, Foxes have lurking holes and the birds of the air have roosts and nests, but the Son of Man has no place to lay His head. Yeshua is looking to put the Mind of Christ and remove our carnal understanding and receive not just truth but revelation of who he is.*

Yeshua was trying to impart to them Revelation of understanding first. First is denying yourself, dying to self and repenting and confessing always and then accepting his teachings how. Ephesians 3; 2 surely you have heard about the administration of God's grace that was given to me for you, 3 that is, the mystery made known to me by revelation, as I have already written briefly. 4 In reading this, then, you will be able to understand my insight into the mystery of Christ, 5 which was not made known to people in other generations as it has now been revealed by the Spirit to God's holy apostles and prophets.

The Devil's main accusation that he evolves in mostly is Generational and also the accuser, to accuse you of your marriage, finances, relationships, prosperity etc. Every time God blesses you religious spirits within man accuses and asks why and how did you get this. Deep within them they are not pleased to see you prosper and grow wealthy in health. Yeshua death and resurrection is indisputable, he was wounded for our transgressions, bruised for our iniquities and by his 39 stripes we are healed. Do not dispute his original intent for us. Except it and embrace it with all assurance that he became poor that we may become rich. The crown of Thorns represented poverty and lack, he took it for us. So right now I rebuke and curse discourse and disorder out of my life in Yeshuas name!. The problem with Christians they accept accusation, even jobs wife brought accusation against him. You buy into the accusation, you speak as one of the foolish, you except your ungodly soul ties. Then you start accusing yourself when they accuse you. Your door to the Supernatural is the impossible all things are possible, if you remove facts and statistics, you will have no way and means to judge the impossible.

Impossible is rooted like a tree in reason, logic and common sense. Till you come to the end of your reason you will never see God! You will be looking always for something else. Give me the desire to come to the end of reason in Yeshuas name. Hunger will cause you to place or make a demand on God Himself! Isaiah 45:11 Thus saith the LORD, the Holy One of Israel, and his Maker, Ask me of things to come concerning my sons, and concerning the work of my hands command ye me. Reason does not understand or accepts how the Supernatural works. You reason and become analytical about everything that has to do with God. Revelation is an Intellectual property and only the Holy Spirit has the Patent to it. Where there is revelation there is the now and the move of God. In the body of Christ you are hearing the self-help Gospel with emotions and feelings, but no demonstration of power because it's being worked by the soul of man and gift not with the Leading of the orchestration of the Holy Spirit.

Hebrews 2:8 and put everything under their feet."[b][c]In

putting everything under them,[d] God left nothing that is not subject to them.[e] yet at present we do not see everything subject to them. The Economic battle ground is reason, Satan bestowed two things Pride kicked out of heaven ego, self-ambition me myself and I. Second when he came to Earth he sowed the seed of Reason to Eve, when you reason with yourself and your situations you're working the curse, how, what, when, where how and why attitude. Now Saints I'm going to launch you back into the Realm of Glory which is before time that means time is subject under your feet.

Genesis 3: Now the serpent was more subtle *and* crafty than any living creature of the field which the Lord God had made. And he [Satan] said to the woman, Can it really be that God has said, You shall not eat from every tree of the garden?2 And the woman said to the serpent, We may eat the fruit from the trees of the garden,3 Except the fruit from the tree which is in the middle of the garden. God has said, You shall not eat of it, neither shall you touch it, lest you die.4 But the serpent said to the woman, You shall not surely die,5 For God knows that in the day you eat of it your eyes will be opened, and you will be like God, knowing the difference between good and evil *and* blessing and calamity.6 And when the woman saw that the tree was good (suitable, pleasant) for food and that it was delightful to look at, and a tree to be desired in order to make one wise, she took of its fruit and ate; and she gave some also to her husband, and he ate. Satan sowed the seed of reason, we reason when it comes to Holiness, obedience, resist the devil and he will flee, instructions, wisdom, understanding, life etc.

We Reason because of our Insecurity issues hello. We

reason when it also comes to acceptance, responsibility, discipline and divine order and repentance. In the name of Yeshua I curse the the curse of reason off of me in Yeshuas name. Eve had two sons at first Genesis 3:4 Adam[a] made love to his wife Eve, and she became pregnant and gave birth to Cain.[b] She said, "With the help of the Lord I have brought forth[c] a man." 2 Later she gave birth to his brother Abel. Now Abel kept flocks, and Cain worked the soil (Ground means Doctrine Twisted with reason). One was the Shepard of animals kept flocks, Cain worked the Soil. You notice Cain the one born of Reason first, worked the soil, where did false doctrine come from. The seed of Cain, he migrated toward a city where the nephelims were a city of giants and fallen angels dwelled. You heard a quote sow your seed in good soil; most soil contains the curse of reason within. There is a Spirit of Reason that embraces compromise, common sense and logic.

Genesis 19:30 Lot and his two daughters left Zoar and settled in the mountains, for he was afraid to stay in Zoar. He and his two daughters lived in a cave. 31 One day the older daughter said to the younger, "Our father is old, and there is no man around here to give us children—as is the custom all over the earth. 32 let's get our father to drink wine and then sleep with him and preserve our family line through our father." The curse of Reason is a generational curse.

33   That night they got their father to drink wine, and the older daughter went in and slept with him. He was not aware of it when she lay down or when she got up.
34   The next day the older daughter said to the younger, "Last night I slept with my father. Let's get him to drink wine again tonight, and you go in and sleep with him so

we can preserve our family line through our father." 35 So they got their father to drink wine that night also, and the younger daughter went in and slept with him. Again he was not aware of it when she lay down or when she got up. The Spirit of reason speaks and is a Generational curse. Genesis 16:16 Now Sarai, Abram's wife, had borne him no children. But she had an Egyptian slave named Hagar; 2 so she said to Abram, "The Lord has kept me from having children. Go, sleep with my slave; perhaps I can build a family through her." Abram agreed to what Sarai said. 3 So after Abram had been living in Canaan ten years, Sarai his wife took her Egyptian slave Hagar and gave her to her husband to be his wife. 4 He slept with Hagar, and she conceived. The Curse of Reason flows through the bloodline.

Galatians 4:4 what I am saying is that as long as an heir is underage, he is no different from a slave, although he owns the whole estate. 2 The heir is subject to guardians and trustees until the time set by his father. 3 So also, when we were underage, we were in slavery under the elemental spiritual forces[a] of the world. 4 But when the set time had fully come, God sent his Son, born of a woman, born under the law, 5 to redeem those under the law, that we might receive adoption to son ship.[b] 6 Because you are his sons, God sent the Spirit of his Son into our hearts, the Spirit who calls out, "Abba,[c] Father." 7 So you are no longer a slave, but God's child; and since you are his child, God has made you also an heir. Yeshua was born out of Divine Promise not Reason.

Galatians chap 4:21 Tell me, you who want to be under the law, are you not aware of what the law says? 22 For it is written that Abraham had two sons, one by the slave woman and the other by the free woman. 23 His son by the slave woman was born according to the flesh, but his son by the free woman was born as the result of a divine promise. One was born of a curse of slave that means subject under the law of mankind. Another born of Divine covenant everything subject under Yeshuas feet.

[24] These things are being taken figuratively: The women represent two covenants. One covenant is from Mount Sinai and bears children who are to be slaves: This is Hagar. 25 Now Hagar stands for Mount Sinai in Arabia and corresponds to the present city of Jerusalem, because she is in slavery with her children. 26 But the Jerusalem that is above is free, and she is our mother. 27 For it is written:

"Be glad, barren woman, you who never bore a child; shout for joy and cry aloud, you who were never in labor; because more are the children of the desolate woman than of her who has a husband."

28 Now you, brothers and sisters, like Isaac, are children of promise. 29 At that time the son born according to the flesh persecuted the son born by the power of the Spirit. It is the same now. 30 But what does Scripture say? "Get rid of the slave woman and her son, for the slave woman's son will never share in the inheritance with the free woman's son."[f] 31 Therefore, brothers and sisters, we are not children of the slave woman, but of the free woman. When you reason you're working the curse and become a slave to the church and body of Christ even when you Tithe, opens the door to reason also. The slave and her son is the Root of a Generational curse called Reason. Meaning if you believe that your cursed because you don't give a Tithe or Tenth that's called reason.

The Spirit of Influence

The spirit of influence is one of the most wiley, yet most destructive, spirits by which the devil is deceiving souls in these last days. It comes so beautifully clothed, having the appearance of just what every saint wants—the power to win souls—and its awful Spirit-quenching power is so completely hidden that thousands of souls have been deceived by it, have embraced it, and are being bound for eternal night.

This influential spirit brings up his arguments so logically, shrewdly, and scripturally (the devil knows the scriptures) that the unsuspecting but zealous soul is completely captivated. He begins his reasoning's about this way....

"You know the true way is so far different from what most people know that you must be very careful in giving them the truth. Don't give them too much at once; feed them on milk; lead them gradually." This is very good. Next he says, "Use much tact and wisdom, for he that winneth souls is wise. Be careful not to say anything that will offend. Pad well the hard hailstones of truth. Teach first on the truths that don't touch their pride and worldliness, and get them to admiring these truths; then when you must come to things that will touch and hurt them, be sure they are in the right mood to receive it. Be very certain that it is the right time and occasion and pray for much wisdom and tact to present it in the right way. Be careful to lead up to it in an easy way from step to step, and if you find they are resenting it, stop; for there is no use to offend unnecessarily. If they become offended, it is sure you never can win them," reminds this influential spirit.

This spirit also gets you to using much human influence in your effort to win souls more rapidly. "Pat them on the back," says he. "Make them feel quite at home; show them how pleased you are to have their presence; talk very nice to them; avoid anything unpleasant or personal. Also, let them have a little part in the meeting; it will please them, and it can't do any harm. If they testify, say amen boldly, even though you know they are not saved. If they are sectarian ministers, let them take the service now and then and lead in prayer.

"Then, when you are in their company, don't be in a strait-jacket about your talking, for there are plenty of good things to talk about besides salvation. If they are witty and inclined to jest, you can laugh with them and put in a little now and then yourself, so they won't feel peculiar and uncomfortable in your presence. Should they invite you to go any place that might be questionable to the old-fogey saints, go, asking no questions for conscience's sake. Then, when there, don't be a spectacle and make the company uncomfortable by your peculiarity or manner of dress. You never can win people if you don't ease up on some of those cranky, fanatical notions of former days," continues this influence spirit.

"Then you must not dress so peculiar; you must seek to be unnoticeable in your dress. So you must narrow (and shorten) your skirt considerably. Don't be worldly—oh, no, never—but don't wear any out-of-date hat, and make your clothes neat and plain, but try to get that smart, bandbox air about all your apparel, and then its lack of trimmings won't be noticed so much. In fact, there is no use in being so cranky. The Bible says modest, and it is modest and plain to have a little lace or embroidery around the neck and sleeves and such necessary places.

"Then you know, those people who are getting somewhat interested are of the better class, and many of the saints are of the common class, so you must be very careful how you speak to and associate with them in public places where this better class might see, for if you make yourself so friendly with the common people, the better class will have nothing to do with you and you never can win them." Thus this deceiving spirit of influence leads you on step by step. You follow on, never suspecting in your zeal and delight in winning souls, how far, far away you have gotten from the Bible method and the Bible highway. When questioned, you vehemently declare that you are not compromising, that it is an awful thing to be fanatical, and that these methods are perfectly lawful. The Bible says nothing against them, and they are a mighty power in winning souls, "For see how many souls are getting saved since we began to use common sense, wisdom, and tact in winning them."

Ah, dear deluded soul, entrapped and being dragged down to hell while trying to win souls, **know you not that souls can never be won to Christ but by lifting up Christ?** Do you not know that doing evil that good may abound will never bring souls to Christ? Do you not know that using the devil's methods to do Christ's work will not be accepted of Him? (2 Corinthians 6:14-15). Doing things for Christ that are contrary to Christ will never win souls. "And I, if I be lifted up from the earth, will draw all men unto me."* If you really want to win souls for Christ, shun not the offense of the cross (Galatians 5:11). Lift Him—in all His humility and world-hated virtues—up to the gaze of sinful men. "No man can come unto me, except the Father which hath sent me, draw him."* It is the Father, not some great human influence, who draws souls to Christ. All who are drawn by the influence are drawn, not to Christ, but to men. The fruits of this spirit of influencing people to accept the gospel are many:

1.   Respect of persons; "But if ye have respect of persons, ye commit sin."*
2.   Pride, which slips in along with respect of person, as you exercise extreme carefulness in your attitude toward the different classes.
3.   Worldliness, as you put on this little extra in your apparel.
4.   Deceit, hypocrisy, and dishonesty in you're putting on false appearances, in flattery, in pretending to live and behave in certain ways in accordance to the opinions of the one you wish to win.
5.   Idle words and foolish talking, but for "every idle word that men shall speak, they shall give account thereof in the day of judgment."* (See Ephesians 5:4.)
6.   Fear of men. God says, "Fear ye not the reproach of men, neither be ye afraid of their reviling's."* "Be not ye the servants of men."*
7.   Quenching the Holy Spirit. This is done by substituting human wisdom and worldly influence for the divine wisdom and leadings of the Holy Spirit. God's ways are not man's ways; neither are his thoughts, our thoughts (Isaiah 55:8).
8.   Withholding God's truth when He said, "Preach the word; reprove, rebuke, exhort."* May God help all who would really be His servants to "renounce the hidden things of dishonesty,"* to rebuke and resist the spirit of influence in their lives, and to live and work for God in God's way.

he spirit of influence is a compromising spirit whose face is toward the world, and who steadily lowers the gospel standard so that people can get on easier without having to forsake so much— not to die so completely to self. Instead of seeking God for more of His power and for His confirmation of the Word through signs and wonders, as did the apostles, this worldly spirit goes down to Egypt for help and depends on the arm of flesh, on the wisdom and influence of men, for its power to win souls. "Therefore shall the strength of Pharaoh be your shame, and the trust in the shadow of Egypt, your confusion."

It is absolutely useless, yea, terribly dangerous, to lower the standard to get people on it, and then try to lift it up to where it ought to be. The people will get on, all right, when the standard is lowered, but when the lifting begins, notice what happens. The raising of the standard is resented, rebuked, fought against, and either you must yield and let it back down and repent for having tried to lift it up, or else you must get off and get back yourself to where you belong. But if you persist in trying to lift it up with all those people on it, you will find, as it is raised, that they were tied to the world and to self by cords of pride, covetousness, love of adornment, amusement, preeminence, etc., and they will be pulled off of the standard and hurled back into the world. This you cannot endure unless you are consecrated to do a work for God, even if there are only two or three who measure to God's holy standard.

This spirit subjects itself to Deceitfulness, pretending to be your friend or brother or sister in Christ. Meaning saying things like yes and amen agreeing with you but not with a genuine motive or intent. It's just enough to keep you locked in the circle or circumference of the ministry. Sort of like a Dr. Heckle and Jyde spirit. Making you feel comfortable that their on your side. Stretching the truth just enough to make others feel their accepted, making them feel appreciated for self-gain and control. This spirit of influence carries spirit of religion causing and attacking your self-esteem and confidence, telling you, you need more training or discipleship. The leaders contradict what they speak of like dying to yourself completely, but allow and pick and choose who to honor and disregard who's in gods council and who is not. This spirit tells you you're not ready to be released or sent out until you submit to my council and rule and reign over your heart body mind and soul.

Prostituting your Character and Personality to win the souls of others to build their kingdom and receiving their Honor ship by receiving the money of extortion for self-gain. Making you feel accepted to win them more money and building their empire for themselves. Most of you cannot discern the Motive and Intentions of the Heart because you're so bored and lonely looking for ministry to be involved in and want a piece of the action no matter what. That's how insecure or bored you really are you will accept bribes and compromise to fit in no matter what. This extortion of flattery is considered the False Angel of Light Character that almost 99% of all Christians cannot discern do to their ignorance or insecurity issues. All they see is gift and anointing within the vessel and have a projection of self-destructive insight when they see people or prosperity or money or some form of habitation of increase they truly believe their own delusion that's genuine. They cannot see the Motive and intentions of a Person's heart. Even if the Ministry or person offers them a position or money of False Hospitality wining and gaining the favor of their hearts for self-gain.

How you can you break or acknowledge this spirit or their intentions and motives, well for one ask the Holy Spirit to show you, and be ready and prepared to make a decision to cut off ungodly soul ties no matter what, without judge in them. When you make an offering in any ministry pray and speak to your offering and say whatever is hidden in darkness reveal it to the light and I lose the spirit of truth on their tongues in Yeshuas name. The truth will be laid out bare they will slip and fall on their own tongue and speak it out in plain their true intentions and motives. Whenever you in a service declare and decree let not my soul enter in their council nor let my glory unite in their wicked assembly. Also speak and declare and decree let the Human Spirit, religious spirit and the Human will be subject under the Power of the Holy Spirit. Saints remember one thing, if you do not cut off ungodly soul ties after truth of their motives and intentions of their hearts are revealed, you are participating in their schemes no matter how loving it may seem this or these spirits actually impregnate with you cause your involved and participating like a third party.

1 Corinthians 10:21 You cannot drink the cup of the Lord, and the cup of demons: you cannot be partakers of the Lord's table, and of the table of demons. The spirit of influence is a drink that corrupts your spirit and heart.
Saints lets move on, In the book of Revelation 6 verse: [12] I watched as he opened the sixth seal. There was a great earthquake. The sun turned black like sackcloth made of goat hair, the whole moon turned blood red, [13] and the stars in the sky fell to earth, as figs drop from a fig tree when shaken by a strong wind. [14] The heavens receded like

a scroll being rolled up, and every mountain and island was removed from its place. 15 Then the kings of the earth, the princes, the generals, the rich, the mighty, and everyone else, both slave and free, hid in caves and among the rocks of the mountains. [16] They called to the mountains and the rocks, "Fall on us and hide us[f] from the face of him who sits on the throne and from the wrath of the Lamb! 17   [g] For the great day of their wrath has come, and who can withstand it?"

Earthquake in Hebrew ragaz: to be agitated, quiver, quake, be excited, perturbed. It also means commotion, or confusion. The father is confusing the enemy and setting his own trap by putting his foot in his mouth. Also your going to see Christians their motive and intentions of their hearts gurgitate, spit up whats in there hidden. Meaning to tell on themselves openly. Black in Hebrew means Shemesh- Battlements, On a castle, fort, or other military fortification, a battlement is the top part of the wall that looks like teeth and it's where soldiers were protected during "battle" upon the castle. You notice a mouth has teeth to bite or to speak, Heavy Prophecy of Yah's fire of his word shall come forth at the tip of our tongues.

Sackcloth in Hebrew means Saq, shaqaq; properly, a mesh (as allowing a liquid to run through), i.e. Coarse loose cloth or sacking (used in mourning and for bagging); hence, a bag (for grain, etc.) -- sack(-cloth, -clothes). Now what sort of grain of meat of revelation are you applying also is your inner character of righteousness being transformed dying to self . Watch this Leviticus 11:32 And upon whatsoever *any* of them, when they are dead, doth fall, it shall be unclean; whether *it be* any vessel of wood, or raiment, or skin, or sack, whatsoever vessel *it be*, wherein *any* work is done, it must be put into water, and it shall be unclean until the even; so it shall be cleansed. The father is pouring out a New Baptism of his spirit within his righteous, a new purification and launching us into deliverance and physical healing. He is revealing an awesome presence of his fire and demonstration of his power.

ANTHONY MONTOYA

CHAPTER 5

There is a new joy and laughter and peace, security you never known that's is going to remain permanently and you're not coming out of it. This is his promise that he is giving us. There is a alignment of strong preparation taking place within the body of Christ. Tents are constructed of black goat hair. "*Dark am I....dark like the tents of Kedar, like the tent curtains of Solomon.*" (SS 1:5). The hair is spun into strands which are then woven together forming panels approximately 2 feet wide and the length of the tent. Over time, the panels begin to bleach from exposure to the sun and are periodically replaced. Very little is discarded as much work is invested in their materials including the tent. The pieces of the tent which are removed are recycled into walls or mats. Another Hebrew letter derived from the tent itself is the letter "chet", a word meaning "wall". This letter in the ancient pictographic script is, a picture of a wall as can be seen in the above picture.

The size of the tent will depend on the size and wealth of the family. The wealthier families will have separate tents for the wife, such as Abraham had for Sarah. As the family grows, additional panels are added to increase the size of the tent. "*Enlarge the place of your tent, stretch your tent curtains wide, do not hold back; lengthen your cords, strengthen your stakes*" (Isaiah 54:2).

The father is releasing wealth and enlargement of our territories considerably to a degree exceedingly great above and beyond our comprehension. We are being spiritually cleansed our cloaks are being remade into something that once was Immortality like it was in the garden of Eden. Moon in Hebrew keseh appointed time, his righteous justice on mankind. This means even death is at hand, it states the stars of heaven fell to the earth, meaning men of great titles God reminded mankind there nothing but dust of this earth. Fig is considered fruit, shaken by strong wind, false doctrine. Then it states every Mountain and island was removed from its place. This means every high thing like pride or what you received spiritually and also island means water or knowledge that was given or have drunk was removed if its not of God. Island AHL **A)** Na % (aN% AN) ac: **?** co: **Ship** ab: **Where:** A ship searches through the sea for a distant coastline (of an island or mainland) in search of the produce for trade. The fig tree produces fruit that is desirable and prolific, since the fig is green and blends in with the leaves, the fruit must be searched out. The searching may result in success or failure. If your Fruit does not increase within character, you are cursed and result in failure. If you have not received and applied hidden manna of revelation either of his new wine the ships of his treasure will not find you, like his favor. There is a new shift and a ship or an ark gathering looking for an island of revelation.

2 Chronicles:21 For the king's ships went to Tarshish with Huram's servants; once every three years the ships of Tarshish came bringing gold, silver, ivory, apes, and peacocks.22 King Solomon surpassed all the kings of the earth in riches and wisdom.

Ivory in AHL **Strongs #3462: AHLB#: 1474-L (V).1474)** Ns % (sN% ShN) ac: **Sharp** co: **Teeth** ab: **?:** The pictograph s is a picture of the teeth, the n is a picture of a seed representing continuance. Combined these mean "teeth continue". The two front teeth are sharp and used for cutting foods by pressing down. (eng: shine - from the whiteness of the teeth) **A)** Ns % (sN% ShN) ac: **?** co: **Teeth** ab: **?N$^{m/f}$)** Ns % (sN% ShN) - **Teeth:** [Hebrew and Aramaic] [freq. 58] |kjv: teeth, tooth, ivory, sharp, crag, forefront| {str: 8127, 8128}. He wants us to chew on revelation, also continue speaking his word.

Apes-An Indian origin may be inferred from the fact that the Hebrew qoph, the Greek kebos and the English "ape" are akin to the Sanskrit "kapi", which is referred to the root kap, kamp, "to tremble". The Holy spirit within us will make those against us tremble, a new source of fire a new baptism of His Holy Spirit from Yah the Father. Let me Explain on May 2nd 2015,′ two fighters Paquio and May weather fought, at one point may weather spirit began to tremble and was in fear, even May weathers father said why are you fighting out of fear, why are you afraid. The Holy Spirit scared the religious spirit demon within May weather. A new Fierceness of the Holy spirit.

Peacocks have pinions- Psalms 91:4 He will cover you with his feathers. He will shelter you with his wings. His faithful promises are your armor and protection. So when he sends Peacocks or baboons, he is sending you armor and protection. Hebrew strongs ebrah: a pinion. Peacock Symbolism-The peacock is a symbol of immortality because the ancients believed that the peacock had flesh that did not decay after death. The peacock naturally replaces his feathers annually; as such, the peacock is also a symbol of renewal. I am sending you a new Armour a glorified body of Resurrection just like Yeshua. Romans 6:5 For if we have been planted together in the likeness of his death, we shall be also *in the likeness* of *his* resurrection.

Here is some more Revelation, you notice it says Peacocks with an S more than one. I am sending you Immortal gifts that come along with it. Let me give you some illustration of what the Father is speaking of Saints, Jeremiah 33: 6 "Nevertheless, I will bring health and healing to it; I will heal my people and will let them enjoy abundant peace and security. 7 I will bring Judah and Israel back from captivity[b] and will rebuild them as they were before. 8 I will cleanse them from all the sin they have committed against me and will forgive all their sins of rebellion against me. 9 Then this city will bring me renown, joy, praise and honor before all nations on earth that hear of all the good things I do for it; and they will be in awe and will tremble at the abundant prosperity and peace I provide for it.'

How would someone tremble before thee, only if they had some Immortal gifts from Heaven here on Earth and it was permanent to stay here with you, well did not Perseus receive Immortal gifts from Heaven. Just being symbolic in this phrase for you to have an understanding of whats to come. Perseus received a sword of extreme power also a horse with wings etc. A young man was Prophesied 8 years ago by a Prophetess in Louisiana, stating there is a Ranch that's yours and there is a horse that has wings and waiting for your arrival here on earth and the Horse can fly!

Let's begin Saints Psalms 10:1: Why do You stand afar off, O Lord? Why do You hide Yourself, [veiling Your eyes] in times of trouble (distress and desperation)? Ancient Hebrew lexicon **1244)** ⯑⯑⯑ (⯑⯑⯑ KN) ac: **Stand** co: **Root** ab: **Sure:** The pictograph ⯑ is a picture of the open palm, the ⯑ is a picture of a seed. Combined these mean "opening of a seed". When the seed opens the roots begin to form the base of the plant by going down into the soil. The plant rises out of the ground forming the stalk of the plant. A tall tree can only stand tall and firm because of the strong root system which supports it.

The root of his word in Revelation, we become the opening of the seed, then we allow the word of his revelation began to root within us and drop within the soil of our hearts body mind soul and spirit. **Strongs #2243: AHLB#: 1163-A (N) 1163** 󠀀󠀀󠀀 (󠀀󠀀󠀀 HhB) ac: **Hide** co: **Bosom** ab: **Refuge:** The pictograph 󠀀 is a picture of a wall. The 󠀀 is a picture of a tent or house. Combined these mean "wall of the house". The walls of the house enclose the home as refuge for the family. A refuge functions as a place of hiding from any undesirable person or situation. **A)** 󠀀󠀀󠀀 (󠀀󠀀󠀀 HhB) ac: **?** co: **Bosom** ab: **?:** A place where one is hidden in the arms and cherished.

Isaiah 40:11 Like a shepherd He will tend His flock, In His arm He will gather the lambs And carry them in His bosom; He will gently lead the nursing ewes. That means only if you are in the Bosom of Yeshua the place of correct nurturing.

Listen as he unveils his revelation in times of distress, Isaiah 49: **16**See, I have engraved you on the palms of my hands; your walls are ever before me. The Bosom of Yeshua a place of Nurture. [17] O Lord, You have heard the desire *and* the longing of the humble *and* oppressed; You will prepare *and* strengthen *and* direct their hearts, You will cause Your ear to hear,[18] To do justice to the fatherless and the oppressed, so that man, who is of the earth, may not terrify them any more!.

The earth and opening of the Sixth seal has opened the

Earth cries out for Justice of Yah. You notice it specifically states so that man, who is of the earth, may not terrify them anymore. There is a shift of complete rest and security only to those who was willing to die to completely to self.

Isaiah 49: **22**This is what the Sovereign Lord says: "See, I will beckon to the nations, I will lift up my banner to the peoples; they will bring your sons in their arms and carry your daughters on their hips.**23**Kings will be your foster fathers, and their queens your nursing mothers. They will bow down before you with their faces to the ground; they will lick the dust at your feet, Then you will know that I am the Lord; those who hope in me will not be disappointed." **25**But this is what the Lord says: "Yes, captives will be taken from warriors, and plunder retrieved from the fierce; I will contend with those who contend with you, and your children I will save.**26**I will make your oppressors eat their own flesh; they will be drunk on their own blood, as with wine. Then all mankind will know that I, the Lord, am your Savior, your Redeemer, the Mighty One of Jacob." Luke 20:34 Jesus replied, "The people of this age marry and are given in marriage. 35 But those who are considered worthy of taking part in the age to come and in the resurrection from the dead will neither marry nor be given in marriage, 36 and they can no longer die; for they are like the angels. They are God's children, since they are children of the resurrection. 37 But in the account of the burning bush, even Moses showed that the dead rise, for he calls the Lord 'the God of Abraham, and the God of Isaac, and the God of Jacob.'[b] 38 He is not the God of the dead, but of the living, for to him all are alive." The tabernacle age of Immortality Saints wake up a new dawn of creation.

Romans 8:18 I consider that our present sufferings are not worth comparing with the glory that will be revealed in us.

19 For the creation waits in eager expectation for the children of God to be revealed. 20 For the creation was subjected to frustration, not by its own choice, but by the will of the one who subjected it, in hope 21 that[h] the creation itself will be liberated from its bondage to decay and brought into the freedom and glory of the children of God. Once we received a glorified body the earth will no longer decay but illilume in Glory.

22 We know that the whole creation has been groaning as in the pains of childbirth right up to the present time. 23 Not only so, but we ourselves, who have the first-fruits of the Spirit, groan inwardly as we wait eagerly for our adoption to sonship, the redemption of our bodies. 24 For in this hope we were saved. But hope that is seen is no hope at all. Who hopes for what they already have? 25 But if we hope for what we do not yet have, we wait for it patiently. This verse speaks of the Redemption of our Glorified Bodies.

Ok in the bible recorded in the day of his death and resurrection everyone has acknowledged three men were crucified that day. Actually four men were crucified that day Judas Iscariot was hung on a tree in the Potters field. Matthew 27:6 The chief priests picked up the coins and said, "It is against the law to put this into the treasury, since it is blood money." 7 So they decided to use the money to buy the potter's field as a burial place for foreigners. 8 That is why it has been called the Field of Blood to this day. 9 Then what was spoken by Jeremiah the prophet was fulfilled: "They took the thirty pieces of silver, the price set on him by the people of Israel, 10 and they used them to buy the potter's field, as the Lord commanded me."[a] You notice it stated a place of foriegners and strangers.

Isaiah 64:8 But now, O LORD, thou *art* our father; we *are* the clay, and thou our potter; and we all *are* the work of thy hand. So the potters field is place of what, Breaking, this Revelation is an interpretation of Broken messages, impartial doctrine. What burial are you being buried into.
You all continue to be Instructed by a false religious witchcraft of false Tithe Doctrine. Lets Recap where this is coming from, Malachi 1: 6 "A son honors his father, and a slave his master. If I am a father, where is the honor due me? If I am a master, where is the respect due me?" says the LORD Almighty.

"It is you priests who show contempt for my name.

"But you ask, 'How have we shown contempt for your name?'

7 "By offering defiled food on my altar.

"But you ask, 'How have we defiled you?'

"By saying that the LORD's table is contemptible. 8 When you offer blind animals for sacrifice, is that not wrong? When you sacrifice lame or diseased animals, is that not wrong? Try offering them to your governor! Would he be pleased with you? Would he accept you?" says the LORD Almighty.

9   "Now plead with God to be gracious to us. With such offerings from your hands, will he accept you?"— says the LORD Almighty.

10   "Oh, that one of you would shut the temple doors, so that you would not light useless fires on my altar! I am not pleased with you," says the LORD Almighty, "and I will accept no offering from your hands. 11 My name will be great among the nations, from where the sun rises to where it sets. In every place incense and pure offerings will be brought to me, because my name will be great among the nations," says the LORD Almighty. Useless fire what kind of fires on the altar, this place is a sacrificial blood offerings. James 3:5 Likewise, the tongue is a small part of the body, but it makes great boasts. Consider what a great forest is set on fire by a small spark. 6 The tongue also is a fire, a world of evil among the parts of the body. It corrupts the whole body, sets the whole course of one's life on fire, and is itself set on fire by hell. So when you compromise the word of Yah and Prostitute yourself in word in flattery your entertaining idol worship of spilt human blood sacrifice and not of Yahs ordinances or Yeshua's interpretation.

12 "But you profane it by saying, 'The Lord's table is defiled,' and, 'Its food is contemptible.' 13 And you say, 'What a burden!' and you sniff at it contemptuously," says the LORD Almighty.

"When you bring injured, lame or diseased animals and offer them as sacrifices, should I accept them from your hands?" says the LORD. 14 "Cursed is the cheat who has an acceptable male in his flock and vows to give it, but then sacrifices a blemished animal to the Lord. For I am a great king," says the LORD Almighty, "and my name is to be feared among the nations. What Illustration is this being introduced as, when you bring an injured animal or diseased animal to Yah. What Kind of Reverence are you showing and whats hidden behind this reverence.

Malachi 2: 2 "And now, you priests, this warning is for you. 2 If you do not listen, and if you do not resolve to honor my name," says the LORD Almighty, "I will send a curse on you, and I will curse your blessings. Yes, I have already cursed them, because you have not resolved to honor me. 4"Because of you I will rebuke your descendants[a]; I will smear on your faces the dung from your festival sacrifices, and you will be carried off with it. 4 And you will know that I have sent you this warning so that my covenant with Levi may continue," says the LORD Almighty. 5 "My covenant was with him, a covenant of life and peace, and I gave them to him; this called for reverence and he revered me and stood in awe of my name. 6 True instruction was in his mouth and nothing false was found on his lips. He walked with me in peace and uprightness, and turned many from sin.

7 "For the lips of a priest ought to preserve knowledge, because he is the messenger of the LORD Almighty and people seek instruction from his mouth. 8 But you have turned from the way and by your teaching have caused many to stumble; you have violated the covenant with Levi," says the LORD Almighty. 9 "So I have caused you to be despised and humiliated before all the people, because you have not followed my ways but have shown partiality in matters of the law." You notice it stated Partiality in the Torah of truth Broken messages. The Place of Judahs Ischariot burial, whats more significant of this Revelation in this passage lets move on. Continued in verse 17 You have wearied the LORD with your words. "How have we wearied him?" you ask.By saying, "All who do evil are good

in the eyes of the LORD, and he is pleased with them" or "Where is the God of justice?"

Malachi 3:6 "I the LORD do not change. So you, the descendants of Jacob, are not destroyed. 7 Ever since the time of your ancestors you have turned away from my decrees and have not kept them. Return to me, and I will return to you," says the LORD Almighty. "But you ask, 'How are we to return?'8 "Will a mere mortal rob God? Yet you rob me."But you ask, 'How are we robbing you?'" In tithes and offerings. 9 You are under a curse—your whole nation—because you are robbing me. According to Tithe it means a portion of a whole, which means Reverenceh whole Heartedly in all thy ways, offering means what is the Motive and Intent of your Suffering, Humility or Stepping near to the Cross or Using Yeshua's spilt blood message for what Purpose in your Heart.

Your cursed when your Motive and Intentions of your heart are Wicked and filled with Deceit etc. Oh Really your asking yourself what do you mean. OK Judah s spirit, deceit and treachery False Humility and angel of Light Spirit. Job 1:6 Now there was a day when the sons of God came to present themselves before the LORD, and Satan came also among them.

8And the LORD said unto Satan, Whence comest thou? Then Satan answered the LORD, and said, From going to and fro in the earth, and from walking up and down in it. You Notice in the Spirit Realm we sit at a table in the midst, All generals were there but only Yeshua himself could see or Discern Satan the Angel of Light spirit sitting there with his gifts and talents. Yah created the gifts and the talents.

Matthew 26: **20**When evening came, Jesus was reclining at the table with the Twelve. **21**And while they were eating, he said, "Truly I tell you, one of you will betray me."**22**They were very sad and began to say to him one after the other, "Surely you don't mean me, Lord?"**23**Jesus replied, "The one who has dipped his hand into the bowl with me will betray me. **24**The Son of Man will go just as it is written about him. But woe to that man who betrays the Son of Man! It would be better for him if he had not been born."**25**Then Judas, the one who would betray him, said, "Surely you don't mean me, Rabbi?"Jesus answered, "You have said so." Now Saints they were at the Table eating, they were eating in what form?(Portions). Tithe Means Portion of a whole.

You Notice the False Humility or angel of spirit is Extremely cunning and difficult to be detected. The 11 Apostles were even blinded themselves. That is the Understanding to ask the Holy spirit to show the motive and intentions ofthe Heart and what spirit is bbeingoperated when someone speaks. Luke 22: 3 Then entered Satan into Judas surnamed Iscariot, being of the number of the twelve. 19 And he took bread, and gave thanks, and brake it, and gave unto them, saying, This is my body which is given for you: this do in remembrance of me.20 Likewise also the cup after supper, saying, This cup is the new testament in my blood, which is shed for you.21 But, behold, the hand of him that betrayeth me is with me on the table.22 And truly the Son of man goeth, as it was determined: but woe unto that man by whom he is betrayed!23 And they began to en quire among themselves, which of them it was that should do this thing.

When they took communion this was another form of

SEEK THE MOTIVE AND INTENTIONS OF THE HEART!

Reverence to Yeshua and Yah. Tithes means Reverence and when you do things in Portions, do it Whole Heartedly. Offerings means more than one, (Motive & Intent) while you're doing it. So your cursed when your portions of Reverence (What false teachings or being spilt out of your mouth and also your portions, (Gift and talent within you).   Also when your offerings (Motive and Intentions) is twisted or Sour its Displeasing to Yah.

One of Satan's decrees are nothing but Hell Mocking Gods unity of words. Romans 6:4Therefore we have been buried with Him through baptism into death(Old Self), so that as Satan was redeemed from the dead(His Fall) through the glory of the Himself, so we too might walk in Debauchery of life. 5For if we have become united with Him in the likeness of His death, certainly we shall also be in the likeness of His resurrection, 6knowing this, that our old self was renewed with Him, in order that our body of sin might remain with, so that we still be slaves to sin(Him Satan). One of Hells Chants, You notice they were four men that were buried that day, In the beginning you had Angel of Light spirit in the Garden of Eden, then you had Jezebel spirit in the book of Kings, then you had the Absalom spirit, King Davids son betrayed him and tried to turn over his own fathers kingdom, then you have Judas spirit in the New testament. In Hebrew you have the four levels of Jewish Interpretation. You have the Pa shat-simple form of understanding literally or natural. Then you have Remetz- hinting of understanding or a deeper truth than what is portrayed. Then you have Drash- searching further, farther is a definition that relates to distance, further is a definition of degree a higher Honorable ground of achievement. Then you have Sod which is Hidden Revelation Prophetic Insight of grandeur of Yah.

Saints Check this out, **PaRDeS: THE FOUR LEVELS OF JEWISH INTERPRETATION OF THEIR SCRIPTURES: The Hebrew/Aramaic word PARDES is spelled in Hebrew and Aramaic without vowels as PRDS. PaRDeS refers to a park or garden, esp. the Garden of Eden. The word appears three times in the Aramaic New Testament (Lk. 23:43; 2 Cor. 12:4 & Rev. 2:7). The letters of Four words PRDS. Luke 23:43** Jesus answered him, "Truly I tell you, today you will be with me in paradise." This is the Garden of Eden Immortality, higher form of understanding here and now withing us, a place of learning still. Yah is not speaking of Heaven yet we need to get through some Universities still, 1,000 year reign back to the Garden of Eden. 2 Corinthians 12 I must go on boasting. Although there is nothing to be gained, I will go on to visions and revelations from the Lord. 2 I know a man in Christ who fourteen years ago was caught up to the third heaven. Whether it was in the body or out of the body I do not know—God knows. 3 And I know that this man—whether in the body or apart from the body I do not know, but God knows— 4 was caught up to paradise and heard inexpressible things, things that no one is permitted to tell. Revelations of understanding that were or are so profound and genuine and too pearly to speak of to swines. Revelation 2:7 Whoever has ears, let them hear what the Spirit says to the churches. To the one who is victorious, I will give the right to eat from the tree of life, which is in the paradise of God.

Saints we are eating from the Revelation of the Tree of Life. When Adam and eve were kicked out of the garden how many years did Adam live, Genesis 5:5 Altogether, Adam lived a total of 930 years, and then he died. He was not permitted yet to eat of the tree of life or Revelation yet, through an act of obedience not to touch it. Hello Adam lived still almost 1,000 years out of the Garden, those who are victorious are going back to the Garden of Eden and live out 1,ooo year reign as an immortal here on earth. What Satan meant for evil God turns it around for his good will and Pleasure. Genesis 50:20 As far as you're concerned, you were planning evil against me, but God intended it for good, planning to bring about the present result so that many people would be preserved alive. Gods original Intent was to give us what Adam and Eve missed out on and by his sovereign mercy and grace he has given back. We are about to experience Paradise and be given whats never been heard of or recorded or received yet since the beginning in the garden.

If some of you are looking or waiting for Armageddon to take place, in Hebrew Arma means high mountains a dwelling, and meggido means a place of crowds. Lexicon :: Strong's H4023 - *Mĕgiddown (Zech. 12:11). Judges 5:19 they fought the kings of the Canaanites. The great battle is the High place of*

False teachings coming to destroy or come against the General spirits of the Fallen angels the Territorial spirits. Megiddo or Megiddon = "place of crowds". **Revelation 16:16** - *And he gathered them together into a place called in the Hebrew tongue Armageddon.*

Matthew 24:21 - *For then shall be great tribulation, such as was not since the beginning of the world to this time, no, nor ever shall be. The battle is the Dwelling place where people come to as great crowds to gather but what spirit is operating certain religions or terrortireswithing* *vessels, countries etc.* **Isaiah 13:9** - *Behold, the day of the LORD cometh, cruel both with wrath and fierce anger, to lay the land desolate: and he shall destroy the sinners thereof out of it. The heavenly father is sending his wrath and destruction here and now.*

Genesis 1:1 In the beginning God created the heavens and the earth. 2 Now the earth was formless and empty, darkness was over the surface of the deep, and the Spirit of God was hovering over the waters. Psalms 97: Clouds and thick darkness surround him; righteousness and justice are the foundation of his throne. God is Light and Dark. The father is speaking of himself in an incomprehensible way! What is high place as he stands of who he is, Righteousness Love, Peace Holyness etc. What is beneath him or his footsteps?, His footsteps are justice. The spirit of the God Hovering over the waters Righteousness, darkness was over the surface of the deep, himself Justice. The deeper you fall in love with him the more Justice comes your way in a Favorable way.

Genesis 1:3 And God said, "Let there be light," and there was light. 4 God saw that the light was good, and he separated the light from the darkness. 5 God called the light "day," and the darkness he called "night." And there was evening, and there was morning—the first day. The father unveiled himself to reicieve him as a secret or mystery because his ways are what?. Romans 11:3 O the depth of the riches both of the wisdom and knowledge of God! how unsearchable *are* his judgments, and his ways past finding out! You can only search if the gift is given to you by his mercy and grace everything is a gift.

Daniel 2: He revealeth the deep and secret things: he knoweth what *is* in the darkness, and the light dwelleth with him.

Isaiah 45:3 (ASV) *and I will give thee the treasures of darkness, and hidden riches of secret places, that thou mayest know that it is I, Jehovah, who call thee by thy name, even the God of Israel.*

Isaiah 61:8 For I, the LORD, love justice, I hate robbery in the burnt offering; And I will faithfully give them their recompense And make an everlasting covenant with them. Isaiah 30:18 Therefore the LORD longs to be gracious to you, And therefore He waits on high to have compassion on you For the LORD is a God of justice; How blessed are all those who long for Him.

Job 34:12 "Surely, God will not act wickedly, And the Almighty will not pervert justice.

Deuteronomy 32:4 "The Rock! His work is perfect, For all His ways are just; A God of faithfulness and without injustice, Righteous and upright is He.

Psalms 99:4 The strength of the King loves justice; You have established equity; You have executed justice and righteousness in Jacob.

Psalms 9:7-8 But the LORD abides forever; He has established His throne for judgment, And He will judge the world in righteousness; He will execute judgment for the peoples with equity.

Revelation 20:12-13 And I saw the dead, the great and the small, standing before the throne, and books were opened; and another book was opened, which is the book

of life; and the dead were judged from the things which were written in the books, according to their deeds. And the sea gave up the dead which were in it, and death and Hades gave up the dead which were in them; and they were judged, every one of them according to their deeds.
Isaiah 66:24 "Then they will go forth and look On the corpses of the men Who have transgressed against Me For their worm will not die And their fire will not be quenched; And they will be an abhorrence to all mankind."

Colossi ans 3:25 For he who does wrong will receive the consequences of the wrong which he has done, and that without partiality.

2 Thessalonians 1:8-9 dealing out retribution to those who do not know God and to those who do not obey the gospel of our Lord Jesus. These will pay the penalty of eternal destruction, away from the presence of the Lord and from the glory of His power,

Deuteronomy 10:18 "He executes justice for the orphan and the widow, and shows His love for the alien by giving him food and clothing.

Psalms 140:12 I know that the LORD will maintain the cause of the afflicted And justice for the poor.

Psalms 146:7-9 Who executes justice for the oppressed; Who gives food to the hungry The LORD sets the prisoners free. The LORD opens the eyes of the blind; The LORD raises up those who are bowed down; The LORD loves the righteous; The LORD protects the strangers; He supports the fatherless and the widow, But He thwarts the way of the wicked.

1   Samuel 24:15   "The LORD therefore be judge and decide between you and me; and may He see and plead my cause and deliver me from your hand."
Romans 12:19 Never take your own revenge, beloved, but leave room for the wrath of God, for it is written, "VENGEANCE IS MINE, I WILL REPAY," says the Lord.

Job 34:18-19   Who says to a king, 'Worthless one,' To nobles, 'Wicked ones'; Who shows no partiality to princes Nor regards the rich above the poor, For they all are the work of His hands?

2   Chronicles 19:7 "Now then let the fear of the LORD be upon you; be very careful what you do, for the LORD our God will have no part in unrighteousness or partiality or the taking of a bribe."

CHAPTER 6

Saints let me give you two more wonderful Revelations, one is the Power of Worship and revelation according to Hebrew and the Power Lending, the different interpretations of sow and giving in complete different formats to understand revelation and truth. The True Revelation of Worship and the Power of Prostration of Power and Honour you can give a Diety! When you give up the Worship not the Honour we think we should give him by opening our mouths.

Worship in Heberew, shachah: to bow down, bow self-down, crouch, fall down flat, humbly beseech, do reverence, Prostrate

A primitive root; to depress, i.e. Prostrate (especially reflexive, in homage to royalty or God) -- bow (self) down, crouch, fall down (flat), humbly beseech, do (make) obeisance, do reverence, make to stoop, worship. Did it say to sit, did it say to stand, Does it say to sing Hello!

Worship Greek proskuneó: to do reverence to (From pros and a probable derivative of kuon (meaning to kiss, like a dog licking his master's hand); to fawn or crouch to, i.e. (literally or figuratively) prostrate oneself in homage (do reverence to, adore) -- worship. proskuneó: to do reverence to

I go down on my knees to, do obeisance to, worship.. Satan was the Number one Worshipper in Heaven and he New the Most Heaviest Reverence of Honour and the Power of Prostration. Our Own Enemy gave us a Secret.

Revelation 4:10 The four and twenty elders fall down before him that sat on the throne, and worship (Prostrated themselves before him) him that liveth for ever and ever, and cast their crowns before the throne, saying!

You have Eulogy worship, Ritual worship and Obedience Worship. Matthew 4:23 [21] "Woman," Jesus replied, "believe me, a time is coming when you will worship the Father neither on this mountain nor in Jerusalem. [22] You Samaritans worship what you do not know; we worship what we do know, for salvation is from the Jews. [23] Yet a time is coming and has now come when the true worshipers will worship the Father in the Spirit and in truth, for they are the kind of worshipers the Father seeks. [24] God is spirit, and his worshipers must worship in the Spirit and in truth." There is a difference and great understanding in Truth!

Psalms 100:4 Enter into his gates with thanksgiving, *and* into his courts with praise: be thankful unto him, *and* bless his name. When you enter into the judges building that's the gates the outer court, then inner courts is where your seated to be seen by a judge, while he seats on his chair in the Inner court. The judge has a private chamber that we are never allowed to see or enter are we. Judges have their private chambers. So when you enter in the Holy of Holies Yawehs Presence in his Chambers in True Worship, you bow down and Prostrate yourself and don't make a peeping sound, Complete Reverence is Mind, body, soul, spirit and all actions in complete silence!

Matthew 4:8
Again, the devil took Him up on a very high mountain and showed Him all the kingdoms of the world and the glory

(the splendor, magnificence, preeminence, and excellence) of them. 9 And he said to Him, These things, all taken together, I will give You, if You will prostrate Yourself before me and do homage *and* worship me.

Satan new the Power of Prostration! Were not letting Yah come in fully and completely, When a judge walks in a court room in the inner courts we stand when he sits, we sit and are in complete silence. How can Yaweh fully come in when we don't all in unity Prostrate ourselves on the floor before him! Matthew 15: **21**Leaving that place, Jesus withdrew to the region of Tyre and Sidon. **22**A Canaanite woman from that vicinity came to him, crying out, "Lord, Son of David, have mercy on me! My daughter is demon-possessed and suffering terribly."

23Jesus did not answer a word. Yeshua did not say a word and stood Quiet! So his disciples came to him and urged him, "Send her away, for she keeps crying out after us." You notice Yeshua never answered her a word or acknowleged her at all.

24He answered, "I was sent only to the lost sheep of Israel." The lost sheep of Israel know how to Prostrate themselves before me.

25The woman came and knelt before him. "Lord, help me!" she said. She knelt down at her masters feet and Prostrated herself before him!

26He replied, "It is not right to take the children's bread and toss it to the dogs."**27**"Yes it is, Lord," she said. "Even the dogs eat the crumbs that fall from their master's table." She reverenced him as Master!

28Then Jesus said to her, "Woman, you have great faith! Your request is granted." And her daughter was healed at that moment.

Mark 6:4 **4**Jesus said to them, "A prophet is not without honor except in his own town, among his relatives and in his own home." **5**He could not do any miracles there, except lay his hands on a few sick people and heal them. **6**He was amazed at their lack of faith. He was amazed as their lack of Reverence toward Him as the Master!

Matthew 9: **18**While he was saying this, a synagogue leader came and knelt before him and said, "My daughter has just died. But come and put your hand on her, and she will live." **19**Jesus got up and went with him, and so did his disciples. A church Leader Knelt and Prostrated himself before the Master hello! Amplified version [18] While He was talking this way to them, behold, a ruler entered and, kneeling down, worshiped(Prostrated himself before Him), saying, My daughter has just [l]now died; but come and lay Your hand on her, and she will come to life.

20Just then a woman who had been subject to bleeding for twelve years came up behind him and touched the edge of his cloak. **21**She said to herself, "If I only touch his cloak, I will be healed." She knelt down and touched the edge of his garment the end the bottom of the garment.

22Jesus turned and saw her. "Take heart, daughter," he said, "your faith has healed you." And the woman was healed at that moment.

The Power true Divine Power of Prostration the greek and latin form of Worship was taught to us to open our mouths and dance and Praise him, In Hebrew its Backwards it means to Shut up completely fall down and Prostrate yourself in complete silence! The Worship has been twisted. We have been Praising him and thanking him but not Truly worshipping in the way he wants it.

Yes there is many forms of worship, obedience, servanthood, trusing in him praiseing him for who he is and what he has done for us without expecting anything and several others, but there is one that is a Secret and Mystery That Satan gave away cause he lead the worship in Heaven for billions of Years!

Psalms 29: [1] Ascribe to the Lord, O sons of the mighty, ascribe to the Lord glory and strength. 2

Give to the Lord the glory due to His name; worship(Bow) the Lord in the beauty of holiness *or* in holy array. Holyness is the condtion of the Heart (Body position) and Condition Heart!. He wants us to position us to meet him Face to face nose to nose lips to lips mouth to mouth body to body! Bow Kneel and Prostate in the Beauty of Holiness! Matthew 10:34 Think not that I am come to send peace on earth: I came not to send peace, but a sword. To separate those who are mine are not mine.

Don't be confused when you hear well Yah knows my heart I don't need to worship and bow in that manner! You been taught wrong, you have to come out among them the religious system! Bow down prostrated Your ego,pride,self glory, logic, common sense and reason and get your behind on the floor!

1 Samuel 24: **8**Then David went out of the cave and called

out to Saul, "My lord the king!" When Saul looked behind him, David bowed down and prostrated himself with his face to the ground. King david was the number one Worshiper who wrote the book of Psalms. To bow is Heavens Worship when you give up the worship the Glory Folds it means to rest in Him to bow when you give it all up in Silence!

More Revelation Saints ok! 1 Chronicles 29:20 Then David said to the whole assembly, "Praise the LORD your God." So they all praised the LORD, the God of their fathers; they bowed down, prostrating themselves before the LORD and the king.

Let back up a little Saints 1chronicles 29:**10** David praised the Lord in the presence of the whole assembly, saying, "Praise be to you, Lord, the God of our father Israel, from everlasting to everlasting.**11**Yours, Lord, is the greatness and the power and the glory and the majesty and the splendor, for everything in heaven and earth is yours. Yours, Lord, is the kingdom; you are exalted as head over all.**12**Wealth and honor come from you; you are the ruler of all things. In your hands are strength and power to exalt and give strength to all.**13**Now, our God, we give you thanks, and praise your glorious name.

14"But who am I, and who are my people, that we should be able to give as generously as this? Everything comes from you, and we have given you only what comes from your hand. **15**We are foreigners and strangers in your sight, as were all our ancestors. Our days on earth are like a shadow, without hope. **16**Lord our God, all this abundance that we have provided for building you a temple for your Holy Name comes from your hand, and all of it belongs to you. **17**I know, my God, that you test the heart and are pleased with integrity. All these things I have given willingly and with honest intent. And now I have seen with joy how willingly your people who are here have given to you. **18**Lord, the God of our fathers Abraham, Isaac and Israel, keep these desires and thoughts in the hearts of your people forever, and keep their hearts loyal to you. **19**And give my son Solomon the wholehearted devotion to keep your commands, statutes and decrees and to do everything to build the palatial structure for which I have provided."

20Then David said to the whole assembly, "Praise the Lord your God." So they all praised the Lord, the God of their fathers; they bowed down, prostrating themselves before the Lord and the king.

After King David did this and said a few words, Psalms 100:4 Enter into his gates with thanksgiving, *and* into his courts with praise: be thankful unto him, *and* bless his name. Then he told the Whole Congregation to kneel fall down and Prostrate yourself before the lord (Yeshua & The King Yah).

In 2 Chronicles 20: **5**Then Jehoshaphat stood up in the assembly of Judah and Jerusalem at the temple of the Lord in the front of the new courtyard **6**and said:

"Lord, the God of our ancestors, are you not the God who is in heaven? You rule over all the kingdoms of the nations. Power and might are in your hand, and no one can withstand you. **7**Our God, did you not drive out the inhabitants of this land before your people Israel and give it forever to the descendants of Abraham your friend?

8They have lived in it and have built in it a sanctuary for your Name, saying, **9**'If calamity comes upon us, whether the sword of judgment, or plague or famine, we will stand in your presence before this temple that bears your Name and will cry out to you in our distress, and you will hear us and save us.'

10"But now here are men from Ammon, Moab and Mount Seir, whose territory you would not allow Israel to invade when they came from Egypt; so they turned away from them and did not destroy them. **11**See how they are repaying us by coming to drive us out of the possession you gave us as an inheritance. **12**Our God, will you not judge them? For we have no power to face this vast army that is attacking us. We do not know what to do, but our eyes are on you."

13All the men of Judah, with their wives and children and little ones, stood there before the Lord.

14Then the Spirit of the Lord came on Jahaziel son of Zechariah, the son of Benaiah, the son of Jeiel, the son of Mattaniah, a Levite and descendant of Asaph, as he stood in the assembly.

15He said: "Listen, King Jehoshaphat and all who live in Judah and Jerusalem! This is what the Lord says to you: 'Do not be afraid or discouraged because of this vast army. For the battle is not yours, but God's. **16**Tomorrow march down against them. They will be climbing up by the Pass of Ziz, and you will find them at the end of the gorge in the Desert of Jeruel. **17**You will not have to fight this battle. Take up your positions; stand firm and see the deliverance the Lord will give you, Judah and Jerusalem. Do not be afraid; do not be discouraged. Go out to face them tomorrow, and the Lord will be with you.' "

18Jehoshaphat bowed down with his face to the ground, and all the people of Judah and Jerusalem fell down in worship before the Lord. **19**Then some Levites from the Kohathites and Korahites stood up and praised the Lord, the God of Israel, with a very loud voice. True Worship is to Bow down and fall Prostrate before him, it says they all fell down Fall, kneel and Prostrate Face to Face!

The Power of Prostration is True reverence! 2 Corinthians 6:17 Therefore, "Get away from them and separate yourselves from them," declares the Lord, "and don't touch anything unclean. Then I will welcome you. 2 peter 3:16 just as in all of his letters he spoke about these things, (in which are things difficult for the intellect), which those who are without teaching and unstable, pervert, as also the other Scriptures, to their own destruction.

Revelation 16:21 And there fell upon men a great hail out of heaven, *every stone* about the weight of a talent: and men blasphemed God because of the plague of the hail; for the plague thereof was exceeding great. Hail raining revelation, stone rock is Christ he is full of mysteries and secrets, weight of a talent is a parable and revelation comes in many forms. The Plague of Hail is True heavy Hard Revelation to Digest and swallow and chew! The great falling away is when revelation of Truth pours out Heavily!

Prophetic Movement or Praise and Dance means to be possessed and come into the uttereance and movement of the Holy spirit to be lead by the Holy Spirit. Prophetic dance and Worship is to bring for the the Prophetic of Prophesy and gifts.

Let's read a Revelation about Two sisters.

Luke 10:38-42 Now it came to pass, as they went, that he entered into a certain village: and a certain woman named Martha received him into her house. And she had a sister called Mary, which also sat at Jesus' feet, and heard his word. But Martha was cumbered about much serving, and came to him, and said, Lord, dost thou not care that my sister hath left me to serve alone? bid her therefore that she help me. And Jesus answered and said unto her, Martha, Martha, thou art careful and troubled about many things: But one thing is needful: and Mary hath chosen that good part, which shall not be taken away from her.

Mary sat bowed and knelt before Yeshuas feet and Prostrated herself at his feet! You notice Martha was concerned about Minstry work which is good but Mary chose the Highets form of Reverence to worship and bow and prostrate herself before her Masters feet!
John 12:1-3 Then, six days before the Passover, Jesus came to Bethany, where

Lazarus was who had been dead,[whom He had raised from the dead. There they made Him a supper; and Martha served, but Lazarus was one of those who sat at the table with Him. Then Mary took a pound of very costly oil of spikenard, anointed the feet of Jesus, and wiped His feet with her hair. And the house was filled with the fragrance of the oil. The House was filled with Glory! When Mary bowed and prostrated herself at the Masters feet!.

Ok saints Matthew 2: 11 And they came into the house and saw the young child with Mary his mother; and they fell down and worshipped him; and opening their treasures they offered unto him gifts, gold and frankincense and myrrh.

When Yeshua was a baby our Master and King the three wise men did what? They bowed down, knelt fell prostrate before him in silence and worshipped him, worship means to bow kneel and prostrate in silence! Giving someone all the Honour is too keep totally quite!

Ok saints lets get to the understanding some more. The Cloud and the Glory (Exodus 40:34-38)As soon as the tabernacle was erected -- apparently even before it was dedicated -- God entered his dwelling."[34] Then the cloud covered the Tent of Meeting, and the glory of the LORD filled the tabernacle. [35] Moses could not enter the Tent of Meeting because the cloud had settled upon it, and the glory of the LORD filled the tabernacle." (Exodus 40:34-35) Can you imagine what that was like? Whoosh! The cloud of God's direction moves over the tent and the Shekinah glory of God fills the tent in overwhelming Presence -- so much that Moses couldn't enter until later (Numbers 7:89).

There were two fatalities entering the Holy of Holies that a high priest can receive one is death or Leprosy If he entered in a incorrect manner. **Leviticus 10:8-10 - "Do not drink wine or intoxicating drink**, you, nor your sons with you, when you go into the tabernacle of meeting, lest you die. It shall be a **statute forever throughout your**

generations, that you may distinguish between **holy and unholy, and between unclean and clean**, and that you may teach the children of Israel all the **statutes which the Lord has spoken to them** by the hand of Moses."

The tabernacle of the Israelites was a highly restricted area. Only Aaron and his descendants were allowed inside the tabernacle to offer sacrifices. (Aaron was a Levite— that is, a descendant of Jacob's son Levi. To be a priest, one must be a Levite. On the other hand, not all Levites were priests. Only a particular family of Levites, the Kohathites, could become priests. Other Levites, however, were involved in the maintenance and transport of the tabernacle.) Penalties for violating access to the tabernacle and its contents were so severe as to result in leprosy or death. Certain rituals inside the tabernacle were so specific that improper administration likewise resulted in death (Leviticus 10:1-7).

The revelation of True worship and the power of prostration defined so the Spirit of Glory and fire can come in!

Last the Power of Lending and Revelation in Hebrew. Revelation Anthony Montoya: The power of Lending.

Amram, Izhar, Hebron and Uzziel.   Numbers 3: [19] The Kohathite clans: Amram, Izhar, Hebron and Uzziel. Amram was moses father, Izhar in Hebrew means Izhar = "shining oil" 1) son of Kohath, grandson of Levi, uncle of Moses and Aaron, and father of Korah; progenitor of the Izharites
Hebron in Hebrew means seat associations or **Brown-Driver-Briggs Hebrew Lexicon:** 'ebron Hebron = "alliance" partnership and agreement unity. Relationship Uzziel

Uzziel: "my strength is God," the name of several Israelites Psalms 28: 6, Blessed be the LORD, Because He has heard the voice of my supplication. 7The LORD is my strength and my shield; My heart trusts in Him, and I am helped; Therefore my heart exults, And with my song I shall thank Him. 8The LORD is their strength, And He is a saving defense to His anointed....He is a Defense to His anointed.

Numbers 3;27 To Kohath belonged the clans of the Amramites, Izharites, Hebronites and Uzzielites; these were the Kohathite clans. [28] The number of all the males a month old or more was 8,600.[b] The Kohathites were responsible for the care of the sanctuary. [29] The Kohathite clans were to camp on the south side of the tabernacle. [30] The leader of the families of the Kohathite clans was Elizaphan son of Uzziel. [31] They were responsible for the care of the ark, the table, the lampstand, the altars, the articles of the sanctuary used in ministering, the curtain, and everything related to their use. [32] The chief leader of the Levites was Eleazar son of Aaron, the priest. He was appointed over those who were responsible for the care of the sanctuary.

Well you add 8 + 6 means is 14. Prophetic meaning of 14 in Hebrew strongs dictionary **#0014** אבה 'abah {aw-baw'}
1) to be willing, consent
   1a) (Qal)
      1a1) to be willing
      1a2) to consent, yield to, accept
      1a3) to desire also means to breath after.

Acts 17: 28For in him we live, and move, and have our being; as certain also of your own poets have said, For we are also his offspring.

Numbers 3: [49] So Moses collected the redemption money from those who exceeded the number redeemed by the Levites. [50] From the firstborn of the Israelites he collected silver weighing 1,365 shekels,[d] according to the sanctuary shekel. [51] Moses gave the redemption money to Aaron and his sons, as he was commanded by the word of the LORD. Now you add 1+3+6+5 equals 15, which is a resemblance of 7+8 which he is King of the Sabbath and 8 which is new beginings. This number prophetically means Spiritual and life Ressurection.

• The fifteen years that God added to the life of Hezekiah suffering of a mortal sickness. (Is 38,1-8)
• Saint Paul enumerates fifteen fruits of the flesh: sexual vice, impurity, sensuality, the worship of false gods and sorcery, antagonisms and rivalry, jealousy, bad temper and quarrels, disagreements, factions and malice, drunkenness and orgies. (Ga 5, 19)
• The Hosea prophet bought a prostitute for fifteen shekels of silver. (Hos 3,2) To be resurrection and cleansed of these fruits of the Flesh. Cleansing every residue or dross the timing is now!

Numbers 15:

[37] The LORD said to Moses, [38] "Speak to the Israelites and say to them: 'Throughout the generations to come you are to make tassels on the corners of your garments, with a blue cord on each tassel. [39] You will have these tassels to look at and so you will remember all the commands of the LORD, that you may obey them and not prostitute yourselves by chasing after the lusts of your own hearts and eyes. [40] Then you will remember to obey all my commands and will be consecrated to your God. [41] I am

the Lᴏʀᴅ your God, who brought you out of Egypt to be your God. I am the Lᴏʀᴅ your God.'" Tzitzits In Hebrew

The tassels were never mentioned in my 18 years of ministry it specifically states throughout your generations to come that means future generations.

Mark 6: [53] When they had crossed over, they landed at Gennesaret and anchored there. [54] As soon as they got out of the boat, people recognized Jesus. [55] They ran throughout that whole region and carried the sick on mats to wherever they heard he was. [56] And wherever he went—into villages, towns or countryside—they placed the sick in the marketplaces. They begged him to let them touch even the edge of his cloak, and all who touched it were healed. The edge of his cloak was the tassle or tzitzits. Your sold out to Yeshua and Kingly, Priestly Prophetic which were considered Kohite anointing to walk into the Holy of Holies behing the viel! The edge of his cloak were the hanging tassels Tzitzits.

Thayer's Greek Lexicon: Yeshuas is making us his harp unto to him! Fine tunning and Proper Timing!
Gennesaret = "a harp

Dimensions of fine tunning unlimited! Hebrews 12:22 But you are come unto mount Zion, and unto the city of the living God, the heavenly Jerusalem, and to an innumerable company of angels. Angels give messages, speak for the father, interprations, secrets, mantles, provisions, Defense, food, strength, protection, Healings etc.

Economic Wealth! Proverbs 22:7 The rich ruleth over the poor, and the borrower *is* servant to the lender. Proverbs

19:17   17 He that hath pity upon the poor lendeth unto the LORD, and that which he hath given, He will repay him again. The poor Is those in need, and the church Apostle and Prophets which is of Him, but you shall speak to your seed and giving and say Yeshua I am Lending to you! He becomes the Borrower and you become the Lender cuase of him Within you!

Dueteronomy 15:6 King James Bible
For the LORD thy God blesseth thee, as he promised thee: and thou shalt lend unto many nations, but thou shalt not borrow; and thou shalt reign over many nations, but they shall not reign over thee.

Principles Power of the lender, Interest,arrest,surety, take it all away, a debt to pay back.

I am lending and I want it back on Tuesday! With 7 times more Interest, if you dont pay your liable to be arrested, surety while I am waiting for this I need security and surety that I will never be left without. If you dont give me on Tuesday, father I have now the right, according to your word to Prophecy this wind which of of the spirit to return with all its benefits.

Were not trying to control Yah at all but in this Revelation it states, are you living Holy and heart intent and motive must be pure. Now you have the right to tell the Father I Have been giving my all, now give me back your all that I continue to lay it before you because I am souled out to you!.

Matthew 20:8
English Standard Version even as the Son of Man came not

to be served but to serve, and to give his life as a ransom for many. Yeshua gave his life as an offering of Sacrifice. So only when you live a life as a sacrificial lamb unto him! Losing your life, denying yourself, dying to self!

You want to have control of this Access then Continue to give your all, your heart in it and Keep Lending it to me! So when you give your not giving or borrowing no more your lending it to Yah and he is Obligated to serve you in this matter! He allowes you to become in Control of this acces of Wealth serving you!

Todah In hebrew means giving, From yadah; properly, an extension of the hand, i.e. (by implication) avowal, or (usually) adoration; specifically, a choir of worshippers -- confession, (sacrifice of) praise, thanks(-giving, offering). According to his word it states that you Lendeth unto him! In hebrew Lending-mashsha: lending on interest, usury From nashah; a loan; by implication, interest on a debt -- exaction, He will pay back the Interest on the Loan and Interest on the Debt thats owed to you when your hearts right! When you give you aid that person in aid, but when you Lend, You aid Populations and Nations!.

Give in Hebrew means yahab: to give 2 Corinthians 9: 6 [Remember] this: he who sows sparingly *and* grudgingly will also reap sparingly *and* grudgingly, and he who sows generously [[a]that blessings may come to someone] will also reap generously *and* with blessings. Sowing and giving pertains to roots of righteousness and good fruits like forgiveness and not complaining but with a gratitude heart. Meaning one who sows generously will have joyous life or reap a sourfull life. Your heart in it all when you sow generously with joy!

2 Corinthians 9:7 Let each one [give] as he has made up his own mind *and* purposed in his heart, not reluctantly *or* sorrowfully or under compulsion, for God loves (He [b]takes pleasure in, prizes above other things, and is unwilling to abandon or to do without) a cheerful (joyous, "prompt to do it") giver [whose heart is in his giving]. Thankful Gratitude Heart! Meaning living a life as an offering sacrfice unto him alone! Meaning people live a life out of a system to retain or get something from God, like hes a casino or be faithfull to him like a robot or ritual, not necessarly in the relationship or imtamacy to do all that is required to do what! Hebrews 10:31 English Standard Version

It is a fearful thing to fall into the hands of the living God. Theres three Baptisms of Death you go through first, accepting Salvation to be willing to change and be transformed and turn from your old ways, Second is Baptism Holy spirit and edification of speaking in tongues the process where the Holy spirit can now cut through and burn with fire dying and death process withing you spiritually and naturally letting go of old desire and your own will. Third is the Fire, to be tried through trials and tribulations of all sorts of suffering for Yeshuas sake. Will you be willing to praise him through your valley and shadow of death and fear no evil!

2 Corinthians 9:8 And God is able to make all grace (every favor and [c]earthly blessing) come to you in abundance, so that you may always *and* under all circumstances *and* whatever the need [d]be self-sufficient [possessing enough to require no aid or support and furnished in abundance for every good work and charitable donation]. Surety! His Word states that you will not need any Aid or Support!

Possessing enough.

9   As it is written, He [the benevolent person] scatters abroad; He gives to the poor; His deeds of justice *and* goodness *and* kindness *and* benevolence will go on *and* endure forever! Increases his Territory it scatters Abroad!

10   And [God] Who provides seed for the sower and bread for eating will also provide and multiply your [resources for] sowing and increase the fruits of your righteousness [[e]which manifests itself in active goodness, kindness, and charity].

The Father is speaking about the Heart the fruits of righteousness, the word and the manna revelation. Charity is not cause your already living a life as an offering of sacrfice, charity is lending!

11   Thus you will be enriched in all things *and* in every way, so that you can be generous, and [your generosity as it is] administered by us will bring forth thanksgiving to God. Giving is Gratitude and Praise thanks. Your generosity in the ministry of his Gifts and talents and all things you will be enriched!

12   For the service that the ministering of this (fund) renders does not only fully supply what is lacking to the saints (God's people), but it also overflows in many [cries of] thanksgiving to God. Fund, Funds $$$$ a renders a full supply what is lacking to the saints but it overflows with many cries of thankfullness to him.

13   Because at [your] standing of the test of this ministry,(You will be tested and tried by fire) they will glorify God for your loyalty *and* obedience to the Gospel of

Christ which you confess, as well as for your generous-hearted liberality to them and to all [the other needy ones]. Needy ones many! He is speaking of many not just helping one person in aid. Literally says them. Lending means many!

14 And they yearn for you while they pray for you, because of the surpassing measure of God's grace (His favor and mercy and spiritual blessing which is shown forth) in you. The Representation of Wealth and Secuirty of him within you, they yearn for you while they pray for you. Yearning for you meaning the goodness and love that was shown comes from Yeshua within you, so they yearn for it and they pray for you because their heart for thankfullness within them.

15 Now thanks be to God for His Gift, [precious] beyond telling [His indescribable, inexpressible, free Gift]! A secret and mystery that sometimes that is beyond telling, but hes letting us know its a free Gift!

V)   Bei% (Be%i Y-HB) - **Give:** [Hebrew and Aramaic] [freq. 62] (vf: Paal) |kjv: give, go, bring, ascribe, come, set, take, delivered, laid, paid, prolonged, yielded| {str: 3051, 3052} Yeilded for God loves a Cheerful giver, Meaning Yahweh loves one you lays his self will down, one who yileds to the Holy spirit. Yaweh loves one who does not complain when he lays his self will down but does it cheerfully! When you lay your self will down your been tortued or persecuted dying on the cross, loosing your life and your own will.

VI)   **Strongs #4991: AHLB#: 2451 (a2)**
2451) Ntn% (tN%n NTN) ac: **Give** co: **Gift** ab: **?:** [from: tn - removing]

V) Ntn% (tN%n N-TN) - **Give:** [A generic verb with a wide application meaning to give] [freq. 2008] (vf: Paal, Niphal, Hophal) |kjv: give, put, deliver, made, set, up, lay, grant, suffer, yield, bring, cause, utter, send, recompense, appoint, show| {str: 5414} Suffer. One of the fruits of the spirit is Long suffering.

VI) 2   Corinthians 12:10 King James Bible

VII) Therefore I take pleasure(JOY) in infirmities, in reproaches, in necessities, in persecutions, in distresses for Christ's sake: for when I am weak, then am I strong.

VIII)   **BDB Definition: Nathan Lend!**
1) to give, put, set
1a) (Qal)
1a1) to give, bestow, grant, permit, ascribe, employ, devote, consecrate, dedicate, pay wages, sell, exchange, (lend), commit, entrust, give over, deliver up, yield produce, occasion, produce, requite to, report, mention, utter, stretch out, extend
1a2) to put, set, put on, put upon, set, appoint, assign, designate 1a3) to make, constitute
1b) (Niphal)
1b1) to be given, be bestowed, be provided, be entrusted to, be granted to, be permitted, be issued, be published, be uttered, be assigned
1b2) to be set, be put, be made, be inflicted
1c) (Hophal)
1c1) to be given, be bestowed, be given up, be delivered up.

When you consecrate and yield up yourself unto him he gives you the secrets of his riches. Then and only then you can permit at will by the leading of the Holy spirit of a Return! When you give your all to him and Lend to him, he is obligated to give His all back to you! You become the Expression of who he is! The father becomes the Borrower and you become the Lender!

About The Author

Hello family, I'm just going to give you a brief illustration of my testimony about me and my life In Yahshua. I'm currently divorced over 10 years one daughter, my daughter is 13 one of the greatest life's experiences in my life. My parents are Ministers of the good news for the last 45years experience in the prophetic call and commission. My father's an Apostle and my mother's a Prophetess, who's been used for 17 years. I've been trained under the Holy Spirit and will always be in training, ever since my walk I've been taught to die to self and to lay down my own self will for the sake of the Kingdom for transformation. My biological father left me when I was 11, I had an encounter with God himself, the Father when I was 18 years of age.

One day everyone was gone, my mother had three children I am the middle child, it was around midnight walking around my home. I spoke to myself and stated I was all alone then the phone rang it was weird, then I said hello the voice said" Are you alone" I then said who is this. The voice continued and said "This is your Father, your not alone." Then I said, "ok who is this, stop playing around!" The voice continued and said, "Go to the mirror and then stated are you alone?" Then I said, "Who is this the voice?" Then he continued, "This is your Father in Heaven." I was stunned for that moment and couldn't grasp or understand the situation and my brain went blank.

Since that day, I've been divorced ten years, slept in the streets homeless for about 6 years, kicked out of churches for being too prophetic, slept in houses with ministers who are apostles and prophets that astro projected out of their bodies.

While I have disobeyed Yahweh several times, he allowed me to see the demonic realm and was attacked heavily by my own disobedience, also by other leaders that have mastered the gift inside them using for their own self gain. Trained under the gift of the discerning of spirits, to discern the motive and intents of the hearts of the people around me.

I was just recently pulled out from being homeless, several years ago about 2 ½ to be precise, generational curses broken off from biological father who made a deal with Satan, An apostle prophesied and stated your biological father made a deal with Satan to have the blood of two of his children for promise for money for the rest of his life. My sister was cured from whooping cough there was no cure at that time. I was set free from several demonic spirits that are so real. My walk in ministry was to discern why so much division, only by Yahshua's grace and the Holy Spirit has graced me to understand the spirit of influence & religion using venom of false doctrine and false prophecies that's been impregnated in the hearts of God's children & have been left crippled and shuts down their own immune system.

My present state I'm ordained minister, my belief is to be a life living sacrifice for Yahweh's kingdom , only to be servant to others and help one another reach Yahweh's purpose n destiny in our lives. To unveil the mysteries and revelations of this kingdom age for all his children to be set free from religion, jezebel spirits, spirit of influence, psychology, false hope (false prophesies), rejection, abandonment guilt, shame, control, seared conscious, subconscious, conscious, mesmoratic cells, trauma, familiar spirits, camellia spirits that transforms and changes color, cockatrice spirit, the false god of Prosperity, Fortune & Destiny, mystical influences that general spirits have had dominion over us.

Isaiah 26: 13-14 (AMP) says, "O Lord, our God, other masters besides You have ruled over us, but we will acknowledge *and* mention Your name only.[14] They [the former tyrant masters] are dead, they shall not live *and* reappear; they are powerless ghosts, they shall not rise *and* come back. Therefore You have visited and made an end of them and caused every memory of them [every trace of their supremacy] to perish." This reference speaks of general demonic spirits even with all religious practices, he will even wipe away the memory of them out of us.

Anthony Montoya

BOOKS BY ANTHONY MONTOYA

The Seed Of Resurrection

The Fruits Of Favor And Increase

Apocalypse Encrypted! Revelation Unleashed! - # 1

Apocalypse Encrypted! Revelation Unleashed! – # 2

Seek The Motive And Intentions Of The Heart!

MINISTRY CONTACT INFORMATION

You may contact Anthony Montoya

through the following sources:

Email Address:

Judah1231@yahoo.com

Website:

anthonymontoyas1.weebly.com